Shaw's Settings

The Florida Bernard Shaw Series

UNIVERSITY PRESS OF FLORIDA

Florida A&M University, Tallahassee
Florida Atlantic University, Boca Raton
Florida Gulf Coast University, Ft. Myers
Florida International University, Miami
Florida State University, Tallahassee
New College of Florida, Sarasota
University of Central Florida, Orlando
University of Florida, Gainesville
University of North Florida, Jacksonville
University of South Florida, Tampa
University of West Florida, Pensacola

Shaw's Settings

Gardens and Libraries

TONY JASON STAFFORD

Foreword by R. F. Dietrich

University Press of Florida

Gainesville · Tallahassee · Tampa · Boca Raton

Pensacola · Orlando · Miami · Jacksonville · Ft. Myers · Sarasota

Printed in the United States of America. This book is printed on Glatfelter Natures Book,
a paper certified under the standards of the Forestry Stewardship Council (FSC). It is a
recycled stock that contains 30 percent post-consumer waste and is acid free.

This book may be available in an electronic edition.

18 17 16 15 14 13   6 5 4 3 2 1

Library of Congress Cataloging-in-Publication Data
Stafford, Tony Jason.
Shaw's settings : gardens and libraries / Tony Jason Stafford : foreword by R. F. Dietrich.
pages cm.—(The Florida Bernard Shaw series)
Includes bibliographical references and index.
ISBN 978-0-8130-4498-9 (alk. paper)
    1. Shaw, Bernard, 1856–1950—Criticism and interpretation. 2. Libraries in literature.
3. Gardens in literature. I. Dietrich, Richard F., 1936- II. Title. III. Series: Florida Bernard
Shaw series.
PR5367.S73 2013
822.'912—dc23   2013015094

University Press of Florida
15 Northwest 15th Street
Gainesville, FL 32611-2079
http://www.upf.com

Funding to assist in publication of this book
was generously provided by the
David and Rachel Howie Foundation

To my children, Michele Stafford Levy, Heather Stafford Villalon,
Katherine Stafford Sanchez, Misty Stafford Yard, and Tony J. Stafford, II;
their spouses; and my grandchildren.
My special thanks to Marti Knobloch for her loving support.

CONTENTS

FOREWORD

In recent years the concert readings of Shaw's plays done by the ShawChicago Theater Co. and Project Shaw in New York (by the Gingold Theatrical Group) have convincingly shown that the language of Shaw's plays is
so powerfully evocative that it can stand alone. In these productions, actors with minimal or no costuming standing before microphones on bare
stages, using few or no props, speaking with appropriate facial expressions
and the slightest body movement, deliver Shaw's lines with great effect.
Yet this sort of minimalist production succeeds partly because the words
themselves manage to adequately convey what has been left out, most no-
tably the visual element provided by actors moving about the stage amid
the settings described in the stage directions, which in various ways are
realized in full productions.

That settings are crucial to Shaw's meanings, whether physically present on the stage or suggested to the imagination in readings, has not been
so systematically demonstrated as it is in Tony Stafford's *Shaw's Settings:
Gardens and Libraries*. To achieve this within a single volume, Professor
Stafford has focused on the most meaningful of frequently used settings,
that of gardens and libraries, meaningful especially because of their fre-
quent interrelationships in the same play. From *Widowers' Houses* to *Back
to Methuselah,* Stafford illustrates his thesis in a significant number of representative plays that as well reveal a sequence of development in Shaw's
dramaturgy over his entire career.

Stafford finds in these interrelationships a semiotics of interpretation
that sheds considerable light upon Shaw's dramatic intentions and accom-
plishments as it relates Shaw's particular usages of gardens and libraries to

the larger cultural meanings of such things. Shaw's presentation of his time and place through the actions of human beings in the particular settings of gardens and libraries has provided and will provide readers and playgoers as meaningful and revelatory a view of the Victorian-Edwardian-Georgian world as one could wish for.

R. F. Dietrich
Series Editor

ACKNOWLEDGMENTS

I should like to thank Elaine Fredericksen, professor emerita at the University of Texas at El Paso, for her encouragement through some difficult times. I should also like to thank Maggie Smith, chair of the Department of English at the University of Texas at El Paso, for her guidance. At this same institution, I should also like to thank Brian Yothers, director of English and American Literature, for providing me with a workable class schedule that enabled me to finish this project; Patricia Witherspoon, dean of the College of Liberal Arts, for her professionalism and for creating an environment that appreciates scholarship; and all my colleagues in the Department of English, who have sustained an intellectual and friendly environment that makes research and scholarship easier. I should also like to pay special tribute to the University of Texas at El Paso, which over the past fifty years has fostered, in ways too numerous to mention, my career.

Introduction

The importance of setting in Bernard Shaw's plays has of course been noticed by many, Rodelle Weintraub summing it up by noting that Shaw's "stage directions are often as important as the dialogue itself"[1] and Arthur Ganz going even further by opining that Shaw's "stage directions are more revelatory than the characters' speeches."[2] This exaggerates the importance of setting at the expense of the dialogue; indeed, recent staged readings on bare stages (by ShawChicago and Project Shaw in New York) have shown how the dialogue can stand alone, but perhaps only because that dialogue so brilliantly evokes the setting that it can be left to the imagination to fill in the blanks. As far as this study is concerned, it does not matter how setting is conveyed; whether it is actually viewed or just imagined from a reading experience or from the dialogue's suggestiveness in a performance, Shaw's settings are indeed more than just a location in which the action takes place. They are, rather, integral to the literary and dramatic values and to the very meaning of the play. Actual or imagined, these settings bear close attention.

Even critics who think Shaw prolix have found it difficult to cut the text of his plays without excising something crucial to the development of the play's action, to a clear understanding of its meanings, or both, and cutting the setting, either actually or by deleting words that suggest it in performance, can especially do damage. Now although much Shaw criticism has shown precisely why setting matters, this has been mostly in reference to individual plays, and what has been neglected is a *systematic* attention to setting that exposes the larger significance of that element to Shaw's playwriting as a whole. Thus, the central thesis of the present study, from beginning to end, is that Shaw enlists the powerful visual component of setting to add meaningful dimensions to the other dramatic elements—such as portraying the characters in depth, refining the conflict, creating startling crises, capturing richly suggestive imagery, clarifying the structure, and developing themes—to achieve his own complex, meaningful, and compelling dramas.

Such a systematic study could generate volumes, of course, unless one finds a key pattern that subsumes and represents the whole, a pattern that can be found in representative plays over Shaw's career. Such a pattern, this study reveals, presents itself in the curious frequency of libraries and gardens as settings in his plays and their often subtle interplay. This library-garden pattern adds up, first, to a realization of how tactile and visual this most verbal and intellectual of writers was, and how suggestive and symbolic, rather than direct and explicit, was his evocation of reality. Studying this pattern leads us to a better grasp of how Shaw's movement through dramatic styles, from apparently "realistic" drama to more fantasy-oriented drama, embodied his development of "the playwright as thinker," to use Eric Bentley's famous phrase, and to a better understanding of what Shaw was driving at in toto.

In Shaw's first play, *Widowers' Houses,* the first words of the play, in the stage directions in the first act, are *"In the garden";*[3] the first words of the second act are *"In the library."*[4] Shaw's pairing and contrasting garden and library in his first play foreshadows a practice of his in the major plays for much of his career, for in play after play he often places the setting of one of his acts in either the garden or the library, or, commonly, in both the garden and the library within the same play—and sometimes within the same act. Of course a play has to be set somewhere, and, one may say, gardens and libraries are as good as any other place, but on the other hand, numerous other places could have been used instead of gardens and libraries. But the persistence of such a practice indicates that it is not accidental, randomly chosen, or without significance. Furthermore, this study establishes that Shaw uses gardens and libraries to reveal character and enhance irony (*Widowers' Houses*); to support structure and clarify conflict (*Mrs. Warren's Profession*); to satirize pretense and mock idealism (*Arms and the Man*); to define ego and expose pretense to erudition (*Candida*); to depict the workings of the Life Force and invoke symbolic overtones (*Man and Superman*); to portray poverty and satirize capitalism (*Major Barbara*); to dramatize primal urges and the power of books (*Misalliance*);

to reinforce literary motifs and foreshadow ominous endings (*Heartbreak House*); to ruminate on ultimate and philosophical concerns by means of the original garden (*Back to Methuselah*); and, in all his plays, to cast light on Shaw's underlying intent, which is to create a powerful dramatic experience. While each play listed above is not the exclusive example of each quality listed, Shaw does not, however, use these settings in the same way in any two plays. Rather, he varies his usage as he moves from play to play, giving us numerous Shavian variations on gardens and libraries. This study reveals the astonishing depth and complexity of Shaw's dramatic genius, and its detailed analysis of these two settings, working in tandem, yields numerous fresh perspectives as we move through the plays. Working garden to garden, Shaw began his first play, *Widowers' Houses,* in a garden setting in its opening scene and began the last play of this study, *Back to Methuselah,* in the original garden, the Garden of Eden, with the earth, Adam, Eve, the Serpent, and Lilith present; he also closes that five-play cycle in a garden with the same cast of characters, and along the way (in *Gospel of the Brothers Barnabas*) uses a library as the single setting of that play, in which a garden (Eden) is the main topic of conversation.

Clearly, Shaw uses libraries and gardens in a wide variety of ways, and we gain a sense of the depth, flexibility, resourcefulness, and complexity of his genius just through examining his settings. But perhaps even more to the point, Shaw's widespread usage of libraries and gardens may only be symptomatic of deeper and more personal elements in his unconscious. As a young man lacking in advanced formal education, he was early on determined to educate himself and gain erudition, and books provided him the means for achieving that goal. He spent nearly every day in the Reading Room of the British Museum for almost a decade (what Michael Holroyd called "his club, his university, a refuge, and the center of his life for almost a decade"[5]) and as Shaw himself said, "My debt to that great institution . . . is inestimable."[6] Libraries are an important part of the "furniture" in his head. As for gardens, they may be a reflection of a deeper relationship with nature; his first twenty years in Ireland were spent absorbing the beauty of nature there, a subject—Shaw and nature—about which more work in the future could be done. Once in the great city of London, his only contact with nature, while in the city, would be by means of London's public parks and the private gardens of those who could afford them. Considering the degree of poverty he suffered in his early years in

London, one can only speculate on how he must have reacted as he looked upon the English gardens, those tranquil, natural respites of the more affluent families, with a certain longing, interest, and admiration.

In applying the terms "garden" and "library" to Shaw's plays, a working definition might be useful. The term "garden" in Shaw is used rather loosely, suggesting that one or several characteristics (but not all) are present: outdoors (in all cases); perhaps, or perhaps not, some vegetation (but not necessarily cultivated); some accommodation, in most cases, for humans (a table, chairs, a bench); some type of edifice or demarcation; and exposure to elements. In some cases, it may be a formal English garden (as in *Mrs. Warren's Profession*), in other cases not. For "libraries," the basic requirement is that there be a book or books, whether it is a well-stocked library (such as Roebuck Ramsden's) or a simple bookshelf (as in *Arms and the Man* and *Heartbreak House*).

The Semiotics of Gardens

What does a cultivated garden signify? Without going into a detailed history of the role of gardens in civilization, particularly Western, a brief statement might be useful. Part of the history of humankind involves humanity's separation from nature, a history of destroying nature in order to replace it with human edifices: pyramids, tents, tepees, log cabins, homes, walls, buildings, streets, sidewalks, parking lots, cathedrals, stadiums, malls, towns, metropolises, and all manner of human-built structures, often with little regard to their effect on nature. For those with baser sensibilities, this presents no problem. For those with a higher consciousness, this is viewed as careless and a lack of acknowledgment of human origins. For the civilized mind, even as we destroy nature, we seek, recognizing nature's superiority, to return to it, or to at least protect it and stay somewhat in touch with it, in order to admire it, appreciate it, enjoy it, delight in it, relate to it, respect it, learn from it, and, if possible, try to be at one with it, or at least remind ourselves of our origins and former unity with nature. This of course occurs mainly in an urban context; the agrarian lifestyle is a different matter altogether, whereby one's living is traditionally made through hard labor and toil of the earth out of bare necessity. Ornamental gardens in the city are a luxury and serve a totally different purpose. Thus the cultivated garden is 1) an attempt to remain in touch with nature, 2) an expression of an expanded consciousness, and 3) a sign of one's ability and means to afford and create such a sanctuary. Thus it evolves in the Western world into a status symbol, signifying culture and affluence. In time, it becomes a place of social intercourse, respectability, and acceptance, and a symbol of social achievement and status.

What is of greatest importance, semiotically speaking, is that by Shaw's time and in Shaw's mind, the English garden was a well-ingrained tradition and powerful symbol, a symbol of man's relation to nature, of intellectual and cultural advancement, and of wealth and power, the epitome of social attainment. Shaw's choice of the English garden for many of his settings was not casual or random but a deliberate use of an entity charged with potent significations. A brief scene from Caryl Churchill's *Serious Money* stresses the garden's position in English society:

> ZAC. Why do the British always want land? (In Paris or New York you live in an apartment, why do the English need gardens?)
> JAKE. You're not upper class without it, you're too American to understand.
> ZAC. You don't make money out of land, you make money out of money.
> JAKE. It's a dream. Woods. Springtime. Owning the spring. What's so funny?
> ZAC. Is that your dream?[7]

The Semiotics of Libraries

What do libraries signify? Again, without going into a detailed history of libraries, a few comments are appropriate. To be human is to have intelligence, awareness, language, and an accumulated record, which record, or knowledge, is located in one place, a library, which is available for consultation and access to all. Thus, the concept of the library seems to be almost as old as the human species itself, and the purpose and value of the library has been unwaveringly the same—a repository of the accumulated knowledge of a culture.

Suffice it to say that by the time of the Renaissance, the library as a symbol of knowledge, learning, and culture was well entrenched in Western consciousness, and the same image projects all the way down to Shaw and his use of libraries for his settings and dramatic purposes. Libraries provided access to the Greek and Roman texts that inspired the Renaissance, and the possession of a personal library as a symbol of achievement, enlightenment, and wealth became well established, as exemplified by someone like Cosimo de Medici, whose collection later provided the basis of the Laurentian Library. Of course Gutenberg's invention of moveable type by 1455 propagated accessibility to the printed word, and libraries, public and private, flourished. The establishment and growth of universities also sponsored the growth of library collections and the quest for knowledge. In England, Sir Thomas Bodley contributed to the expansion of the Duke of Gloucester's collection at Oxford University in the late 1500s, and England's largest library, the British Library in the British Museum, Shaw's constant abode for nearly a decade, was founded in 1759. Once Parliament passed the Public Library Act in 1850, libraries sprang up across the island. To Shaw, a poor boy from Dublin, the image of the library, and especially his entrance into the sacred halls of the British Museum Reading Room, must have seemed like an entrance into some magical, awe-inspiring institution that he desired to become a part of. It left an indelible impression on him, and he would successfully become a part of it. His entrance to the world of the library must have been a significant moment in the life of the ambitious and impressionable, but confident, young man.

Thus, somehow, in Shaw's mind, libraries and gardens came to represent the quintessence of achievement of upper-class British society, of that level of social status that he ironically targeted for his assaults on the hypocrisy, pretentiousness, hollowness, superficiality, and irrationality as manifested by the British social system. But gardens and libraries, in Shaw's plays, in themselves do not represent just that element but are used in far more complex and meaningful ways. As a beginning, they provide the backdrop as a way of establishing a certain social level. As Shaw practiced his art over a period of many years, his use of gardens and libraries changed from play to play; sometimes he used them one way, sometimes another; sometimes in concert, sometimes separately; sometimes as symbolic backdrop, sometimes integrated into the fabric of the play. But he always used them to contribute greatly to the play's ultimate effect and meaning.

Theoretical Considerations

The present study approaches Shaw's plays with a bifurcated vision, as both literary texts and as texts intended for performance. It is easy enough to see the literary relationship of gardens and libraries to other literary elements in the text, but it would be an incomplete study were it to ignore how these settings work in performance and what effect they have on the viewing, as opposed to reading, audience.

There exists of course more than one kind of "performance study." On the one hand, performance theory, in general, attempts to be a discipline that embraces folklore, anthropology, theatre, sociology, cultural studies, dance, music, play, games, sports, ritual, language, and so on in terms of human behavior, action, and interaction. Among the notable scholars and practitioners who espouse this definition of performance theory are Richard Schechner, Victor Turner, and Barbara Kirshenblatt-Gimblett in the Department of Performance Studies at NYU, and Dwight Conquergood in the Department of Performance Studies at Northwestern University. As Schechner writes, performance study "draws on and synthesizes approaches from a wide variety of disciplines in the social sciences, feminist studies, gender studies, history, psychoanalysis, queer theory, semiotics, ethnology, cybernetics, area studies, media and popular culture theory, and cultural studies."[8] The present study does not attempt to do all that.

On the other hand, there is a type of performance study that examines a dramatic text for the purpose of discovering how the text basically translates into performance, how it affects the audience, what values it instills on a live stage in a theatre; this is a theory practiced by someone like Raymond Williams, for example, who was concerned with the relation between text and performance. This theory provides some of the foundational considerations of the present study, abetted as well by literary theory approaches. Williams views literary text and theatrical representation not as separate entities but "as the unity they are intended to become," lamenting that the "literary study and theatrical representation are, almost always, in separate compartments."[9] Instead, he is concerned with *"the written work in performance,"*[10] complaining that "a separation between literature and theatre is constantly assumed," yet drama is both literature and theatre, "not the one at the expense of the other, but each *because* of the other."[11]

Williams reminds us that drama "is a work intended for performance, and, similarly, the great majority of performances are of literary works," that "there is a work of literature, the play, which is intended to be performed, but can also be read," and a dramatist writes a "literary work in such a manner that it can be directly performed."[12] The playwright is not only writing a literary work but, "by exact conventions, *writing the performance.*[13] While Williams admits that a separation has been assumed between literature and theatre, "we must not allow ourselves to be persuaded that it is inherent in all drama."[14] Williams maintains that although actors' movements and settings are written in a "single form," speech must contain this form: "not words in front of a background, nor words accompanying movement, but words, scene, and movement in a single dimension of writing."[15] Nor does Williams omit the importance of setting in performance when describing the four elements of drama.

The present study leans heavily on this approach, but its focus narrows to particular settings—libraries and gardens—to examine how setting not only composes much of the literary value of Shaw's plays but also affects their performance. Moreover, by tracing Shaw's use of these settings through some of his major plays, we also discover Shaw's change, adaptability, and dramatic instincts in his use of these particular settings. We shall not overlook the fact that while we are dealing with literary texts with gardens and libraries described therein, in performance these gardens and libraries remain powerfully before the audience's eyes and impress their function and meaning on the live viewer in a live performance.

1

Widowers' Houses

"Life Here Is a Perfect Idyll"

Even though *Widowers' Houses* is Shaw's first play, it has an artistic completeness of conception and a surprising sophistication in style, technique, and content. Some critics, ignoring the artistic issue, have chosen to focus on the satiric and propagandistic elements in the play, labeling it Shaw's "darkest and bleakest" comedy, noting that it is concerned more with "human depravity" rather than the traditional comedic subject of "human folly,"[1] and calling it an "insistent piece of economic propaganda."[2] But others have argued for its artistic qualities, qualities, as McDowell says, that "compensate for the flaws that its detractors . . . have overemphasized."[3] McDowell continues by pointing out that for a beginning playwright, Shaw exhibits an expertise in "directness of approach, subtlety of implication, mastery of the tensely drawn scene, and remarkable terseness and economy of line."[4] Indeed, Shaw himself insisted that *Widowers' Houses* is not a "pamphlet in dialogue" but a "work of art as much as any comedy by Moliere."[5] Shaw was justifiably proud of its artistic worth and was cognizant of the fullness of its conception, of its "viability in the theater," and the "subtlety and the range of implication present in it."[6] This is not to say that the propagandistic element does not make a strong presence in Shaw's play, as it does in all of his plays, and the play is indeed a virulent attack on greed, exploitation, tainted money, hypocrisy, and the class system. But the artistry, while not perfect, also deserves recognition. By examining Shaw's use of the garden and the library in *Widowers' Houses* in meticulous detail, one gains an appreciation of the complexity, subtlety, and mastery that Shaw therein reveals, as well as an insight into the play's deeper textual implications.

As with any viable piece of dramatic literature, critics have noted a number of different themes in *Widowers' Houses*. Some have focused on Shaw's attack on society, on the exploitation of the poor, on slum-landlordism, on greed, and on indifference toward the destitute. Charles Carpenter, for example, notes that the "broad target is the prevalent assumption that capitalism is the best of all possible economic systems," that "poverty and its consequences are inevitable,"[7] and that "the slum mortgagee and landlord are 'powerless to alter the state of society.'"[8] As Marker puts it, "its theme is ruthless exploitation of the destitute and homeless by the mercantile and the upper classes alike," and its intent is "to implicate every member of the audience in that social crime."[9] Carpenter adds that Shaw "puts the blame squarely on society as a whole."[10]

But, on the level of the individual characters, Shaw inculcates an entirely different theme. While the statements that the play makes about society in general, as noted by the critics, are true, a far more stinging indictment arises from the fact that these evils exist because they are supported by a system of hypocrisy and pretense as practiced by those who are trying to gain respect and acceptance into a class that they yearn to be a part of. Thus Shaw uses the settings of gardens and libraries as a means to develop and dramatize in a subtle and powerful way a major theme involving hypocrisy and pretense.

Although the garden and library are merely stage settings, much of Shaw's intent is contained in his stage directions, and his descriptions support and eventually merge with the action and characters. It has long been recognized that Shaw's stage directions contain vital insights, and that, as noted in the introduction to this study, his "stage directions are more revelatory than the characters' speeches."[11] Even as a beginner, Shaw exhibits his determination "from the outset to direct his plays on paper, down to the smallest movement or inflection."[12] In a study of the influence of Shaw's stage directions on a playwright such as Oscar Wilde, Morrison points out that Shaw "continued to develop stage directions into a combination of psychological analysis, political documentary, and philosophical discourse, shaping flesh and blood characters and their whole moral universe, with a vigour and artistry unmatched by any other playwright."[13] The same may be said of his physical descriptions as well.[14] A major working assumption of the present study is that nothing in Shaw is unimportant, and everything down to the smallest detail has significance, such as his use of gardens and libraries, a study of which is rewarded with an understanding of his intent and an awareness of the interrelatedness of all the parts in his plays.

In *Widowers' Houses,* the very first words that Shaw wrote for the dramatic form, preceding the rest of his canon, was *"the garden."* This particular garden happens to be *"the garden restaurant of a hotel at Remagen on the Rhine."*[15] The significance of this garden serves as a prelude to the other gardens he would introduce in later plays. He continues by saying that it is *"a fine afternoon in August."* Again, as will be seen in play after play, the action of Shaw's comedies takes place in splendid weather, a point Shaw always emphasizes. There are rarely storms, clouds, darkness, and oppressive conditions, the one notable exception being the opening scene of *Pygmalion,* which takes place in the rain outside Covent Garden. This is not coincidental but rather an essential part of Shaw's satiric statement. Shaw takes pains to present a surface, in a lovely garden, with delightful weather, pleasant, tranquil, and, almost, an "idyllic" world (Cokane's description), which ironically belies the ugliness underneath, the foulness composed of greed, pretense, falsity, hypocrisy, and selfishness. *Widowers' Houses* initiates the precedent for this. Underneath the pleasant August afternoon in the garden restaurant, the powerful unwritten laws of upper-class British society are at work, here and in any number of gardens later on, and controlling some of the characters in this particular situation.

The nature of a garden (in this case in a foreign country), the inhabitants of the garden, and the attitudes exhibited in the garden are clues to the meaning generated from such a setting. The fact that this particular garden is located in a foreign country with Englishmen there immediately establishes the fact that the people present are tourists and therefore, likely, persons of some means. Present at the beginning are Trench, the nephew of Lady Roxdale, and Cokane, a gentleman who is obsessed with propriety and all the inviolable rules of upper-class England, and the subject of their opening conversation is "appearance," a not uncommon garden topic in Shaw's plays. Cokane, in point of fact, encapsulates the very essence of many of Shaw's gardens where appearances, acceptability, and proper conduct prevail (*Mrs. Warren's Profession* being such an example). Cokane serves as the voice of conventional society in this particular garden. When Trench, who cares little for form and appearances, begins to sing a rousing drinking song, Cokane is scandalized and delivers a scalding reprimand to Trench: "In the name of common decency, Harry, will you remember that you are a Gentleman, and not a coster on Hampstead Heath on Bank

Holiday"; "either you travel as a gentleman, or you travel alone"; "I have been uneasy all the afternoon about what they [the other English couple] must think of us. Look at our appearance."[16] After Trench's casual rejoinder, "what's wrong with our appearance?" Cokane stresses, "how are they to know that you are *well connected* [emphasis added] if you do not shew it by your costume?"[17] Trench concedes, "I suppose I ought to have brought a change."[18] With Cokane's emphasis on social class, appearances, respectability, and proper conduct ("tact" is Cokane's motto), the theme of the garden, as well as the play itself, is established. As shall be seen, through so many of Shaw's plays, the garden is the place where the rules of respectable British society are most powerfully enforced and dramatized, a place where some people already fit in, where some are trying to fit in, where some, while trying to fit in, obviously do not belong, and a place from which some, for example, Vivie Warren, try to escape. It is a place of the ultimate socially acceptable test, as exemplified by Eliza Doolittle in *Pygmalion* when she passes as a duchess at the ambassador's *garden* party.

Cokane presents the very epitome of British garden behavior: formal, proper, prudish, and rule-bound. When Trench, who ironically is the one with the upper-class connections, calls Cokane "Billy," Cokane recoils: "Do drop calling me Billy in public, Trench. My name is Cokane. I am sure they were persons of consequence: you were struck with the distinguished appearance of the father yourself."[19] Later, Cokane, exposing his true values, asks, "how am I to preserve the respect of fellow travelers of position and wealth, if I am to be Billied at every turn?"[20] Also, Cokane, ever the invoker of the aristocracy, turns to Trench, with no seeming motivation, and asks him, within hearing distance of the Sartoriuses, "I have often meant to ask you: is Lady Roxdale"—whose name also connotes a garden, or at least the idea of a pleasant place in nature—"your mother's sister or your father's,"[21] and when Cokane, always knowledgeable about upper-class behavior, suggests that Lady Roxdale "looks forward to floating your wife in society in London" while Trench scoffs at the idea, Cokane tries to instruct him with, "you dont know the importance of these things; apparently idle ceremonial trifles, really the springs and wheels of a great aristocratic system."[22] Cokane, always the picture of politeness, affability, and sometimes archness, as though he himself were a member of the aristocracy, stresses "good manners," "morals," "tact," and "delicacy! good taste! Savoir faire!"[23] In the middle of the act, Sartorius and Cokane depart to visit a church, during which time the audience discovers that Trench and Blanche have already conversed and are in the process of establishing a relationship and sealing it with a kiss, which Cokane witnesses. Alone with him, he berates Trench *"with the severity of a judge"*:

> No, my dear boy. No, no. Never. I blush for you. I was never so ashamed in my life [...]. No, my dear fellow, no, no. Bad taste, Harry, bad form! [...] She a perfect lady, a person of the highest breeding, actually in your arms [...]. Have you no principles, Trench? Have you no religious convictions? Have you no acquaintance with the usages of society?[24]

After Sartorius has requested that Trench receive letters from his family to the effect that Blanche would be acceptable to them, Cokane's sense of etiquette and good breeding shows once again. He knows, for example, that Lady Roxdale will want to know what Sartorius's wealth is derived from. When Trench tries to shrug off such issues, Cokane admonishes him once again: "When will you begin to get a little sense?" Trench asks him not to be "moral," but Cokane reminds him of the rules, asking, "if you are going to get money with your wife, doesnt it concern your family to know how that money was made?"[25] Toward the end of the act, Shaw creates a tableau of Cokane composing a letter to Lady Roxdale on behalf of Trench, trying to put into the most diplomatic and polite language Trench's situation with Blanche. The letter is completed in a meaningful scene of Sartorius dictating some of the words, symbolic of Sartorius's powers of control and the dominance of his voice.

Scholars have of course been intrigued with the implications of Cokane's name. McDowell offers that Cokane's name suggests "a mindless hedonism deriving from a drug-induced lethargy and also a man who is at home in a world of illusion and false appearances, a dweller in the land of Cockaigne,"[26] while Woodfield asserts that his name suggests "Cockaigne, the fabulous land of luxury and idleness, signifying what he represents."[27] But in a garden of aristocratic behavior, what is required is a narcotic to keep ugliness, disturbances, impoliteness, indiscretion, abrasiveness, and real truth at bay, and the drugs that provide this are tact, good taste and manners, delicacy, politeness, diplomacy, and proper conduct, all of which Cokane is a master of. These drugs make social interaction function more gently, softening the harshness of the violations of their codes.

In this same garden of respectability where Cokane lounges, Sartorius dominates by his mere presence (as Blanche says, "everybody is afraid of papa: I'm sure I dont know why"[28]). Although Sartorius is not a member of the aristocracy, he is comfortable in a social setting and a garden because he has cultivated the manner of the upper class, the word *gentleman* being connected with him over a half-dozen times in the first act alone. It is pretense at its fullest, and the garden often is a place of great hypocritical practice. Shaw notes that Sartorius's *"incisive, domineering utterance and imposing style, with his strong aquiline nose and resolute clean-shaven mouth, give him an air of importance."*[29] The impeccable details of his aristocratic dress, appropriate to his name and appearance, are significant: *"He wears a light grey frock-coat with silk linings, a white hat, and a field-glass slung in a new leather case,"* and, Shaw adds, is *"formidable to servants, not easily accessible to anyone."*[30] The message is clear: He is a man to whom appearance, and consequently acceptance, is tantamount, and the name "Sartorius" bespeaks the importance of clothing to him (this in ironic contrast to Trench, a member of the upper class, whose attitude toward dress is quite casual). In short, here and throughout the play, Sartorius behaves as though he is a member of the upper class, even though he is not. When Sartorius's porter places the packages on a table and the waiter tells him that that table is already taken, Sartorius's reaction is extreme and revelatory, speaking *"severely"* and *"with fierce condescension."*[31] When Cokane attempts to smooth things over, Sartorius arrogantly and *"coldly turn[s] his back on him."*[32] He mimics an attitude of privilege and haughtiness and is only too eager to display what titles he can, telling Cokane, "I am a vestryman."[33]

Through the rest of the garden scene, Sartorius displays his determination to gain acceptance through his powerful control, especially by means of Trench's relationship with his daughter, Blanche. Shaw describes her as a *"well-dressed, well-fed, good-looking, strong minded young woman, presentably ladylike,"*[34] a Pygmalion-like creation of Sartorius. Clearly, these two seek entrée into upper-class British gardens, even though their present search is in a foreign garden. In due time, it becomes clear that Trench and Blanche have an attraction to each other, but Sartorius will not let it advance until he has assurance that he will get what he wants. When Sartorius asks Trench if there will be any objections from his family, Trench demurs that his family has nothing to do with it. Sartorius's response reveals his position, his determination, and the importance of upper-class acceptance to him: "Excuse me sir: they have a great deal to do with it."[35] Trench assures him that she will be accepted, but Sartorius says, "that wont do for me, sir," and "I must have a guarantee on my side that she will be received on equal terms by your family."[36] He requires a guarantee that Trench's relatives, belonging to a social class who, in Sartorius's words, "turn their backs on newcomers whom they may not think quite good enough for them,"[37] will not do the same to Blanche. Trench is uncertain how to guarantee such an attitude, but Sartorius knows: "When you can shew me a few letters from the principal members of your family, congratulating you in a fairly cordial way, I shall be satisfied."[38] This is the crux of the play; it is Sartorius's prime motivation, and the essence and symbolic meaning of the garden. Sartorius has pulled himself up from extreme poverty by making a fortune in slum dwellings, and now he craves nothing more in the world than for him and his daughter to be accepted by upper-class society, and it begins in and is defined by the garden.

On the subject of Sartorius's control, several critics have complained that "the entire play is founded on the vast coincidence that on a continental vacation the youthful hero, Dr. Harry Trench, should meet and become desperately infatuated with the daughter of a great slum landlord," who manages the very property from which his income derives.[39] Woodfield calls it "stretching both coincidence and probability; that the father has a connection to the hero through his aunt stretches both even further."[40] This is looking through the wrong end of the lens. Sartorius is not the kind of man who leaves things to chance; it is just as possible, and more than likely, that Sartorius planned this trip with the full knowledge that Trench would be on the same trip, on the same boat, and staying in the same hotel, hoping that nature would take its course, and what appears to be a coincidence may well not be a chance encounter at all. As Sartorius himself tells Cokane, "the truth is, Mr Cokane, I am quite well acquainted with Dr Trench's position and *affairs* [emphasis added]; and I have long desired to know him personally."[41] By his own admission, Sartorius keeps a close eye on Lady Roxdale's family and its "affairs." It is more believable and likely that he has created this situation, and, as would be typical of him, Sartorius may have carefully calculated and anticipated everything: the "chance" meeting of Blanche and Trench, Trench's objection to Sartorius's source of income (even though he could not have foreseen Lickcheese's informing Trench about Sartorius's business, he could have surmised that with the ongoing parliamentary and clerical investigations and the publication of the "blue book," sooner or later Trench would find out), Trench's complicity in the business, and Blanche's reaction.

In a performance of the play, one other graphic depiction of Sartorius's almost puppetlike control, as mentioned previously, is created by the tableau of Sartorius dictating a letter to Cokane, who is writing the letter for Trench that will be sent under Trench's name to Lady Roxdale, who will actually be hearing Sartorius's words when she reads it. Such are the convolutions necessitated by the deceptions of garden behavior. The scene ends with Sartorius reading the letter, which he has just dictated, although Cokane finished it, *nodding gravely over it with complete approval.*[42] The scene displays Shaw's mastery of irony and performance values.

Aside from his desire to amass wealth, Sartorius's most powerful longing is to have his daughter, Blanche, accepted into upper-class society, and his efforts have been designed to create a young lady who will be at home in the English garden environment, even though he appears, through his determined insistence (the old "reaction formation" principle), insecure about her acceptability. When Blanche is reluctant to visit yet another church, Sartorius convinces her by reminding her, "I would like you to see everything. It is part of your education,"[43] a point on which she will not cross him: "Oh, my education! Very well, very well: I suppose I must go through with it."[44] He has gone to great pains and expense to make her well educated and well bred. When Sartorius gives his reasons to Trench about his need for proof of acceptance by Trench's family, he makes a revealing point when he says, "I am resolved that my daughter shall approach no circle in which she will not be received with the full consideration to which her education and her breeding [*here his self-control slips a little: and he repeats, as if Trench has contradicted him*]—I say, her breeding—entitle her."[45] The depth of Sartorius's feelings on the subject is clear. And again, a few lines later, Shaw's directions establish the importance to Sartorius of Blanche's status when Trench says, "Blanche is a lady: thatll be good enough for them" (meaning his family), and Sartorius, *"moved,"* says, "I am glad you think so."[46] Blanche reveals her knowledge of the rules of polite society when she scolds Trench for speaking "to me without any introduction,"[47] and "you had no right to speak to me that day on board the steamer."[48] But her true self lurks just below the surface. Her hypocrisy is unintentionally revealed when Trench reminds her, "it was you who spoke to me,"[49] and again later when Trench says, "here they [Sartorius and Cokane] are back again," and Blanche, her mask almost slipping, starts to curse with "Oh, d—." Again and again we see through the false facade she maintains. A few lines later, when Cokane reprimands Trench for his behavior with her and insists that "she [is] a perfect lady, a person of the highest breeding,"[50] Cokane's words ring hollow.

As for the meaning of characters' names, Blanche's name is obvious, the implication being that it is ironical, since she is anything but pure, but it also conveys her father's attitude toward her and, as a verb, *to blanch* is to whiten, which is what Sartorius has tried to do through her education and breeding. Moreover, there could also be a garden connection, in that "to blanch" is to scald garden vegetables to make them lighter and more flavorful, which is another way of describing the process Sartorius uses.

Critics have assigned various associations to Trench's name. McDowell says that *Trench* "suggests an individual who is 'entrenched' in his society and who becomes a 'blocking' character set against radical change,"[51] while Woodfield notes that "'Trench' has a heavy sound which suggests that his initial *'rather boyish'* manner overlies an unappealing stodginess (he also digs himself a 'trench' from which there is no escape)."[52] Further, Vogeler speculates that by assigning the name of Trench, Shaw "perhaps meant to suggest how entrenched were London's land and tax systems."[53] The name also suggests several other possibilities, culminating in a garden connection. We know first of all that Sartorius selected the villa at Surbiton because, as he says, "I chose the house because it is on gravel. The death-rate is low,"[54] meaning that its good drainage helps prevent the infestations and diseases associated with bogs, sewers, and swamps. We also know that this is in contrast to the conditions in the slums Sartorius owns, for, as Lickcheese says, "you come down with me to Robbins's Row; and I'll shew you a soil and a deathrate, I will!"[55] We also know that a trench is one means by which soil is drained, and we know that in Sartorius's scale of values this is of great importance to him. Perhaps Trench's name signifies Sartorius's expectations of living above the swamp of lower class on a higher, well-drained social level by means of Trench. Second, a trench is also a means by which two bodies of water are connected, or something that connects a body of water to a target area, as Trench will be Sartorius's connecting trench to the aristocracy. Third, although Trench's family is already a member of the aristocracy, a fact that Trench handles with aplomb, Trench, through his name, is nevertheless associated with the garden. A trench is also a means by which a garden is irrigated, and Trench will serve as the means by which Sartorius will grow his own upper-class garden of respectability and acceptability.

One final connection regarding gardens should be noted. When Cokane reads from the Baedeker about Rolandseck, describing it as surrounded with numerous villas and *pleasant gardens* [emphasis added],"[56] Blanche says that it "sounds civilized and comfortable. I vote we go there," to which Sartorius responds, "quite like our place at Surbiton, my dear," and "quite," Blanche concurs.[57] With the introduction of the villa at Surbiton into the text, this passage serves as a bridge to the garden motif in act 2 located at Surbiton.

The garden motif appears again in act 2, but there it is contextualized in such a way as to make a powerful ironic contrast. After Sartorius discharges Lickcheese and leaves the room, Lickcheese is then left alone with Trench and Cokane and proceeds to describe to them, in a discussion of the source of Sartorius's wealth, the abominable conditions existing in the "tenement houses," "houses that you wouldn't hardly look at without holding your nose,"[58] that Sartorius owns and that serve as an ironical contrast to Sartorius's world of gardens and villas. Lickcheese points out the contrast himself: "Just look how he lives himself, and youll see the good of it to him. He likes a low deathrate and a gravel soil for himself, he does." When Cokane invokes the old cliché, "the love of money is the root of all evil," Lickcheese makes the connection for us: "Yes, sir; and we'd all like to have the tree growing in our garden."[59]

When Sartorius returns, he invites Cokane with, "what do you say to a stroll through the garden, Mr Cokane? We are celebrated here for our flowers," to which Cokane replies, "Charmed, my dear sir, charmed. Life here is an idyll—a perfect idyll. We were just dwelling on it"[60]—a blatant prevarication, for what they had just been "dwelling" on before Sartorius entered is the inhumane conditions of Robins's Row. Sartorius, having heartlessly dismissed Lickcheese with haughty indifference, turns to Cokane, the epitome of English garden manners, and invites him into his pleasant garden while Lickcheese faces his four starving children "looking to me for their bread."[61] Sartorius, eager to become accepted into upper-class British society, has acquired, in addition to an aristocratic demeanor, a garden of his own, a garden in which he takes obvious pride, being "celebrated for our flowers." Through the play, Sartorius moves from a tourist's restaurant garden in Germany, in act 1, to a villa with a garden, in the resort place of Surbiton, in act 2, to their house in Bedford Square, London, in act 3—moving all the while through a world of opulence. But the play has a fourth setting, the squalid tenement houses of Robin's Row, which contrasts with Sartorius's settings and incriminates, with biting irony, the pretense, hypocrisy, and foundation on which Sartorius's wealth is founded. In fact, Sartorius will not even go anywhere near his slum properties, for, as Lickcheese phrases it, "catch him going down to collect his own rents! Not likely!"[62] The garden rule again is decorousness, acceptability, respectability, and indifference to the suffering of those less fortunate. Or, as Lickcheese states it, "many another daughter has been turned out upon the streets to gratify his affection for [Blanche]."[63]

In *Widowers' Houses,* Shaw also uses the library, along with the garden, to visually support and develop his purpose. Act 2 begins with the stage directions *"In the library of a handsomely appointed villa at Surbiton on a sunny forenoon in September."*[64] Shaw notes, *"all the walls are lined with shelves of smartly tooled books, fitting into their places like bricks."*[65] The books are obviously of expensive editions, beautifully decorated, of the classics—and untouched (*"fitting into their places like bricks,"* having never been taken off the shelves and "obviously unread," as Marker puts it).[66] When Cokane comments later, "you must be happy here with all these books, Mr. Sartorius. A literary atmosphere," Sartorius, unaware of the irony of his words, says, "I have not looked into them. They are pleasant for Blanche occasionally when she reads."[67] Sartorius's words are belied by Shaw's opening stage directions where Shaw points out that as the scene opens, *"Blanche, in her prettiest frock, sits reading The Queen,"*[68] a periodical that concerns itself with the gossip around the queen's court. Blanche is not interested in the beautiful, tooled classics on the library shelves. They are there, as with so many things in Sartorius's world, for appearances, in this case to give an impression of "education and breeding," which he emphasizes about Blanche's upbringing several times. In *Widowers' Houses,* the library is present for the same reason the garden is, as a powerful and subtle revelation of attitudes in British society, attitudes that spawn appearance, pretense, and hypocrisy.

Since, from Sartorius's point of view, the expensive library is there for Blanche, it is by means of Blanche that the irony and hypocrisy of the situation is presented. While a reader of the printed text of the play may forget these opening stage directions, fading naturally from consciousness as action, character, and dialogue subsequently get more of the reader's attention, a live audience sitting in a theatre facing the stage with the library set in prominent view throughout the act could not let the set slip away so easily. A performance of the play would elicit the irony of the contrast and the incongruity between the setting, an established symbol in Western civilization of learning, education, breeding, literacy, and culture, and the action of the characters, especially as performed by Blanche. As her true character begins to be revealed, the blatant hypocrisy of her behavior is emphasized by the backdrop of culture and enlightenment. Her father tells her at one point, "you will of course not meet him until he has spoken to me," to which she responds *"hypocritically"* (Shaw's description), "of course not, papa. I shouldn't have thought of such a thing."[69] We find out later that Trench has already shown the letters from his family to her before Sartorius sees them, in direct disobedience to her father's command and a sign of her duplicity.

When Trench and Blanche have a conversation alone, and he announces to her that he will not accept money from her father and that they will have to live on his seven hundred pounds a year, Blanche begins, from that point on to the end of the act, to lose all self-control, and her violent temper begins to emerge, right in front of the beautifully tooled books. Shaw traces her progress. At first she fights against it: *"Her face and voice betray the beginning of a struggle with her temper."*[70] When Trench takes her hand away at one point, *"she flushes angrily; and her voice is no longer even an imitation of the voice of a lady."*[71] This is the person who is reputed to be "a perfect lady" and is regarded as such by her father. She tries to win Trench over, her *"voice softening and refining for the last time"*; when that strategy fails, she becomes *"white with anger."*[72] After this, she is out of control, *"too angry to care whether she is overheard or not."*[73]

After she angrily breaks off the relation with Trench, we see her real vicious nature emerge in the scene, in the library, with the parlor maid. She scolds the maid in the most humiliating and cruel way, *"seizing her by the hair and throat"* and shouting, "stop that noise, I tell you unless you want me to kill you."[74] The maid can hardly speak *"as Blanche's fingers tighten furiously on her"* and is saved only by the arrival of Sartorius, who tries to coax Blanche into controlling her temper. In a live performance, the visual irony of Blanche's inhumane behavior being played out in front of "her" library would be evident to an audience. Gardens and libraries in conjunction in Shaw's early plays are used to establish the value of appearance, and the inevitable hypocrisy, to the upwardly ambitious, as Shaw perceived it, in British society.

With no garden or library present, the last act takes place in Blanche's parlor ("this is my daughter's room"), fire burning, curtains drawn, and lamps lighted. Bernard Dukore points out that traditionally the time sequence in comedy is from winter to spring, but that in *Widowers' Houses,* the first act occurs in August, the second in September, and the third in winter.[75] Dukore concludes that "the increasingly bleak seasonal ambience ironically contrasts with the surface gaiety of the play's conclusion, and it supports Shaw's mockery."[76] Sartorius and Blanche have also seemingly withdrawn more into themselves and are now alienated from the world. We have also penetrated deeper into the heart of the Sartorius family, where the truth is revealed about the real and cynical nature of society and their participation in it. Shaw, nevertheless, visually emphasizes again their hypocrisy by noting that the pianoforte has *"a sort of bedspread which covers the top, shewing that the instrument is seldom, if ever, opened."*[77] Everything in the Sartorius household, seemingly, is for appearance's sake.

Since it is January in London in act 3, a garden setting would not be possible; meanwhile, although it is Blanche's parlor and not a library, the book motif is still present, but it resonates in a different way, and it lies at the heart of several motifs and important moments. When Lickcheese returns to Sartorius's house, now as a prosperous investor with a new business proposition about the slum dwellings, he begins by producing a book that contains the results of the Royal Commission on Housing of the Working Class, in which Sartorius is described as "the worst slum landlord in London." Lickcheese *"doubles back the book at the place indicated, and hands it to Sartorius"*[78] (this is how Blanche will discover what the book says about her father). But Sartorius is indifferent to the publication: "I dont care that for my name being in bluebooks. My friends dont read them and I'm neither a Cabinet Member nor a candidate for Parliament."[79] But Blanche a little later discovers the book and reads. The tableau of her as she *"sits down and begins to read"* contrasts with the opening tableau of act 2 where she sits in the library of expensive books reading her popular publication for amusement. Three critical actions result from her discovery of the "bluebook," as the commission's book is called. First, she comes to understand the reason why Trench "would not touch the money" of her father's, which caused her to break off the engagement. She tries to rip the book and, failing that, tosses it onto the fender in the fireplace. Second, the book is the means by which Blanche's duplicitous nature is revealed yet again. As Sartorius looks about for the bluebook, he asks Blanche, "have you seen it?" Blanche, still furious over what she has read, replies, "No. Yes. [*Angrily*] No: I have not seen it. What have I to do with it?"[80] After spying it on the fender, Sartorius, as well as the audience, sees his daughter's duplicity. Third, when Blanche confronts her father about the book, it is an opportunity for her father to explain the rationale of his business, for him to discuss the nature of poverty, and for him to inform her, and the audience, of his own impoverished background. The book provides the occasion for Shaw to practice his "drama of discussion" at this point in the play. It also provides the opportunity for Blanche to express her, and her father's, basic value system: "How can you expect anyone to think well of us when such things are written about us in that infamous book?"[81] In all instances, her true inner self, sitting by the fire in her parlor in the heart of the house, emerges. She states that she "hates" the idea of poverty and does not wish to know about the poor, and announces, "I love you because you brought me up to something better [. . . and] I should hate you if you had not."[82] Not realizing the implications of his own remarks, Sartorius boasts, "I have made a real lady of you," and "it is natural for you to feel that way, after your bringing up. It is the ladylike view of the matter."[83]

The purpose of Lickcheese's visit is to make a business proposal to Sartorius that basically involves fixing up the slum dwellings so that a higher compensation can be gained when they are torn down for highways and other renewal projects. It is the height of hypocrisy, cynicism, and inhumane values and is perhaps best summed up in Sartorius's mendacious statement: "I certainly feel, as Mr Cokane puts it, that it is our duty: one which I have perhaps too long neglected out of regard for the poorest class of tenants."[84]

This statement is put into clearest perspective when compared to the conversation at the beginning of act 2 when Sartorius discharges Lickcheese for spending "one pound four" for fixing a staircase. While *Widowers' Houses* exposes the heartlessness and injustices of British society, it is the underlying hypocrisy and pretense that is really at the heart of the problem, and this is communicated by Shaw's use of gardens and libraries.

Widowers' Houses is a remarkable example of Shaw's dramatic practice of integrating gardens and libraries into the revelation of characters (as well as the implications of their names), the delineation of conflict, the symbolic value of the settings, the establishment of atmosphere, and the development of the theme of pretense and hypocrisy.

2

Mrs. Warren's Profession

The Walled Gardens

Even more so than in *Widowers' Houses,* Shaw relies heavily on the garden setting in *Mrs. Warren's Profession* to accomplish his social commentary, and especially to attack hypocrisy as the underlying cause of society's corrupt value system. In *Mrs. Warren's Profession* the surface object of attack is different from that of his first play, and the garden is far more prevalent: Three acts out of four involve a garden. Thus the garden setting is fundamental to the social commentary and the meaning of the play as revealed through action, character, conflict, structure, and theme. No library is present.

The play was written in 1893, but Shaw had to wait almost ten years before he could get a production of it, and that was only two private performances at the New Lyric Club by the London Stage Society on January 5 and 6 in 1902. The critics, of course, denounced the play for its decadence and immorality. In New York, when it opened at the Garrick Theatre on the night of October 30, 1905, the cast was arrested for disorderly conduct, the play was closed, and one review slammed it as "illuminated gangrene."[1]

In more recent times, scholars generally have agreed that Shaw's prostitution play ultimately is not about prostitution at all. As Charles Carpenter puts it, "prostitution is his real subject only in the sense that it is a glaring symptom of a pervading disease," and it is his subject "in the universal sense of selling oneself to make a living or buying those who must."[2] Dan Laurence calls it a "frontal attack on a smug, greedy society of prostitutes, not merely of whores . . . but [of] industrialists, politicians, clergy, press, [and] country squires . . . , all earning knighthoods, baronies, and social prominence in the process";[3] he states that Shaw's attack is "leveled at the social system," that "all members of society are blameworthy," and Kitty Warren is "an end product of society's guilt," a guilt based on greed for the material.[4] Laurence also compares it to Shakespeare's *Measure for Measure*, wherein all are "caught up in their hypocrisies, greed, lust, perverted sense of values, and superficialities."[5] Arthur Ganz points out that "for Shaw the heart of the matter is not sentiment but money," that Shaw calls into "serious question the ethics of bourgeois society," and that the capitalist system exploits not only female labor but the laboring class in general.[6] Admittedly, as with so many of Shaw's plays, the play is about many things—the evils of capitalism, the limited opportunities for women in Victorian society for self-sufficiency, the exploitation of those on the underside of society, tainted money, social conventions, and acceptability, among other things—but in all these cases, the practice of hypocrisy seems to drive all the other ills.

Shaw was predictably bemused by the self-righteous outcry of his contemporaries. Wrote he, "a really good performance would keep its audience out of the hands of women of the street for a fortnight at least."[7] While his quip sounds as though the play has the moral intent of keeping men "out of the hands of prostitutes," the vital point of his double-edged remark is that the people who were raising indignant voices against his play are the very ones who themselves are active customers of prostitutes. His comment, while aimed at defending the morality of his play, was more targeted at the widespread hypocrisy in society; it also expresses his intent to take the attack on hypocrisy beyond what he had done in *Widowers' Houses*. Shaw is not concerned with the personal issue of prostitution for Kitty Warren (as Laurence says, "Shaw neither defends nor condemns Kitty")[8] but seeks to treat the pervasive presence of hypocrisy in all of society and to expose society's habit of pretending one thing in order to hide something else; the garden becomes a primary instrument in helping him achieve this purpose.

Three of the four acts are located in a garden or eventually involve a garden, and even the fourth gives us a reminder of the garden from which Vivie has escaped. The first words of the stage description establish the scene: *"Summer afternoon in a cottage garden on the eastern slope of a hill."*[9] Further directions emphasize that *"a paling completely shuts in the garden, except for a gate on the right. The common rises uphill beyond the paling to the sky line."*[10] Five features of this setting are repeated, for emphasis, in act 3:

a garden, an enclosing fence, a gate, open space stretching out beyond the fence, and splendid weather. These provide the biting effect Shaw intends as well as contributing to the meaning. In act 1, the commons, the space outside the garden, gain attention by the fact that several entering characters appear on the commons first, and all five arrivals make their entrance through the garden gate (instead of coming in through the cottage). Only Vivie is already in the garden at the beginning; she will be the only one who will exit through a garden gate to the freedom beyond the garden fence, as represented by the open space and the commons. It is Shaw's sense of irony that the surface pleasantness of the weather masks the social darkness beneath it.[11] While act 2 takes place inside the cottage, Shaw does not let the audience forget about the garden. His descriptions make it clear that he has shifted the point of view 180 degrees so that the audience is facing, upstage, the window and door that it had seen from the garden in act 1 *("a fine starlit night without"),* thus stressing the interaction between inside and outside and keeping the garden present. At the beginning of act 2, each character makes an entrance from the garden, by midact characters start exiting into it, and, at the end, after Vivie and her mother have had a candid and cathartic "discussion," Vivie opens the door, comments on the beauty of the night, and *"draws aside the curtains of the window"* to reveal the scene *"bathed in the radiance of the harvest moon rising over Blackdown."*[12] The temporary reconciliation between mother and daughter and the accompanying good feelings are enhanced by the beauty of the scene, Shaw pushing the dramatic pendulum as far as he can go in one direction with the aid of the garden setting. The curtain comes down with the audience looking at the garden, its enclosing fence, and the temptation of the open land of freedom beyond the fence once again, a foreshadowing of what will eventually transpire.

In act 3, Shaw transfers the action to another garden, that of the Reverend Samuel Gardner: *"In the Rectory garden next morning, with the sun shining from a cloudless sky."*[13] A garden wall and gate are again present: *"the garden wall has a five-barred wooden gate, wide enough to admit a carriage, in the middle."*[14] Again, Shaw makes the audience aware of the landscape on the other side: *"Beyond the gate is seen the dusty high* road [emphasis added], *parallel with the wall, bounded on the farther side by a strip of turf and an unfenced pine wood."*[15] Although the act begins with Frank and his father in the garden, action from beyond the wall intrudes. As in act 1, most entrances are through the garden gate, except for Praed, who comes in through the hedge, and soon the reverend announces in great dismay that "Mrs Warren and her daughter are coming across the heath with Crofts"[16]—toward the garden, of course, where the remainder of the action in this act is centered, with garden, wall, gate, and the terrain beyond clearly in view, all under a sunny, *"cloudless sky."*

The garden idea also functions in the play's structure, movement, and crisis. The first three acts highlight the garden setting, while the fourth does not, for the movement of the play takes the action elsewhere, and it is precisely at the main crisis in the garden in act 3 that the movement away from the garden begins. What brings the action to the turning point is that Vivie, from the beginning and up until the end of act 2, resents her mother as long as she excludes Vivie from the secrets of her private life. But when Mrs. Warren explains the impoverishment of her girlhood, which forced her into prostitution, Vivie not only sympathizes with her mother but rejoices in her fortitude: "My dear mother: [...] you are stronger than all England."[17] They reconcile and remain so until Crofts blunders out that Kitty Warren is still in the business, only now as a bawd. Vivie is sickened by the knowledge, the tenuous bond between mother and daughter is severed, and the play moves toward its conclusion. This climactic moment between Sir George and Vivie not only provides information that alters the course of the play, but also contains a link between the garden motif and society's system of pretense that enables Sir George and Kitty Warren to function in acceptable society. Unbeknownst to Crofts himself, his exposition underscores the whole hypocritical basis on which everything operates, noting that the Duke of Belgravia earns some of his rents "in queer ways," the archbishop of Canterbury has a few publicans and sinners among the ecclesiastical commissioners' tenants, and the Crofts scholarship at Newnham is funded by his brother, an MP who has six hundred factory girls not making enough wages to live on.[18] He chides Vivie, "if youre going to pick and choose acquaintances on moral principles, youd better clear out of this country, unless you want to cut yourself out of all decent society."[19] He succinctly summarizes the hypocritical rule of society that "there are no secrets better kept than the secrets everybody guesses."[20] All of England is indicted in his sweeping law of society, and it is a moment of epiphany for Vivie. After Crofts has explained to Vivie, as they sit chatting in a pleasant garden in ironic contrast to the dark undertones of his exposition, the rules of how upper-class society works (the garden rules, as it were), Shaw creates a visual picture in order to draw attention to Vivie's change as well as to initiate the final movement of the play. Incensed with Crofts and what she learns from him about society (which is even more devastating than the discovery of her mother as brothel manager), Vivie seeks flight from the garden: *"She raises the latch of the gate to open it and go out. He follows her and puts his hand heavily on the top bar to prevent its opening."*[21] In performance, it is a breathtaking moment, a coup de grâce, and symbolically captures the garden's significance. They wrangle briefly in this position. Then Frank arrives, Crofts leaves, and Frank tries to entice Vivie, with his game of "babes in the wood," into remaining in the garden. But nothing can stop her exit. "Goodbye," she says to Frank, and when he asks, "where shall we find you?" she announces, standing in the garden's gate, "At Honoria Fraser's chambers, 67 Chancery Lane, for the rest of my life."[22] Vivie's exit through the gate, the effect heightened by Shaw's reserving it until this moment and utilizing it as part of the physical conflict of the scene, marks the basic progress, as well as the actual turning point of the play, and it calls attention to the metaphorical possibilities of the garden motif. The dramatic pendulum, which began with Kitty and Vivie reconciling while looking out on the radiant garden, has now reached its farthest point in the other direction, again aided by the garden's significance. While it may be pointed out that Vivie is headed toward a rather routine, sterile future, calculating actuarial tables in a city office, the more important point is what she is leaving behind, with all its hypocrisy, in the garden of conventionality.

Act 4 is located in the law office of Honoria Fraser at the top of New Stone Buildings, London, with *"the chimneys of Lincoln's Inn and the western sky"* clearly in view through *"a plate glass window."*[23] Through exact geography, Shaw makes it clear that the achievement of the last act is a complete reversal of the first three. The audience now faces westward (or southwestward), looking toward those gardens in Surrey from which Vivie has escaped. The progress of the play, then, and by implication of Vivie, is from those tightly enclosed (*"fence"* and *"wall"*) and carefully controlled (by the mores of the garden) little plots of land of fine homes and country cottages to a city office, a new challenge where social gardens, for Vivie at least, do not exist but freedom does.

Shaw enhances the garden theme by giving all his characters, except for Vivie, names associated with land, especially land that is fenced in and intended for some type of cultivation—in a broad sense, a garden. Although Shaw, to avoid libel allegations, apparently used London street names as a source for some of his characters—in this play, Praed Street and Warren Street for example—he still chose, out of all the streets he could have used, names harmonious with his garden motif. In the case of the title character, it is true that a "warren," as a place designated for rabbit breeding, seems an appropriate name for a prostitute and a brothel keeper, but it is also consistent with the encircled land image, for the first definition of the word in the *Oxford English Dictionary* is "a piece of land enclosed and preserved for breeding of game." Moreover, when Reverend Gardner knew Kitty years before, she was Miss Vavasour, and *vavasour*, a term from the Middle Ages, denotes a person who holds farmland belonging to a superior lord and who has landholders under him (or, as the *OED* puts it, "a feudal tenant").

There may be yet another association with Mrs. Warren and the garden motif. At the beginning of act 2, the first words of the scene are uttered by Mrs. Warren, when she expresses her inner frustration: "O Lord! I dont know which is the worst of the country, the walking or the sitting at home with nothing to do."[24] Why then, one may ask, is she there, except that country gardens are an acceptable place to be? Ganz notes that she "is bored with society" and, ironically, "Vivie is as bored by it as she."[25] Additionally, Mudford states that the play's real villain is the "vice which [Shaw] was most often to attack in all his political writing: the vice of idleness, the 'loafing' life."[26] Both Kitty Warren and Crofts are guilty of this kind of lifestyle, and an English garden is the perfect symbol of such aimless living, where the main activities are drinking tea (or something stronger) and making idle conversation.

Sir George Crofts bears a family name, which, as a generic term, the *OED* defines as "a small piece of arable land adjacent to a house." The Reverent Gardner and his son Frank are associated with the word *garden*, which is explicit and self-evident. The name Praed, while a proper name familiar to the residents of London, exists in the English language in the root of the adjective *praedial*, which means "of or relating to land" or "landed." Since Shaw received his first lessons in Latin from his uncle William George Carroll, "under whose tutelage he advanced to such a degree that upon entering Wesleyan Connexional School he rose almost immediately to the head of his class,"[27] he would have known, in all likelihood, that *praedium* means "farm," or "estate" and perceived its relationship to the garden image and to the other names in the play.

Of course none of the details of their lives or their characters connect them with fenced-in land. None are outdoor, country types, nor are any of them dependent on farming. In fact, they dislike the country and feel more at home in the city. Kitty Warren says, "I'd a good deal rather be in Vienna."[28] Crofts, although of the "landed class," prefers to invest his money in brothels in Brussels, Ostend, and Vienna, where he spends most of his time, while Praed, an architect, is more comfortable among the museums, concert halls, and buildings of the cities of Europe. Only Sam Gardner lives in the country, and that is not by choice but by necessity. The reason behind Shaw's choice of such names, then, must originate more from their metaphorical usefulness than from what they denote.

Through the use of related names, Shaw has linked together all the characters in the play, except Vivie. Moreover, all the members of this group share some common traits and receive similar treatment. Each is guilty of some type of pretension, and all are exposed for their hypocrisy, mostly by Vivie in her quest for honesty. Ironically, while most of them pride themselves on the rejection of cant, they are prone to falsehoods in spite of themselves. In addition, each of the major characters has at least one scene that utilizes the garden setting in a meaningful way, and they all conform to the mores of the garden, to one degree or another.

Praed, an artistic, freethinking type, admits to the pretenses imposed on him by society in his youth, labeling his own behavior as "affected as it could be" and governed by the rule of "always saying no when you meant yes."[29] But he does believe in beauty. Vivie, however, thinks of cultural pursuits as phony and gives Praed several examples of why she thinks so. Praed is astonished at her attitude, but in act 3, when Praed extols the beauty of Brussels and Ostend, she is vindicated: These European cities that he holds up as models of Western culture are the very ones where Vivie's mother operates her brothels. Beauty among such degradation, Vivie feels, can only be hypocritical, and Praed's belief in art is exposed as such by her biting cynicism.

The candor implied in Frank Gardner's first name is belied by the garden overtone of the second. Although he tries to be unpretentious and brutally frank, especially with his father, his insistence on "love's young dream" is scorned by Vivie as an illusion, and his desire to play the garden game of "babes in the wood" and to be "covered up with leaves" is jeered at by Vivie: "Ah, not that, not that. You make all my flesh creep."[30] Moreover, while he may like Vivie for the person she is, he also likes her mother's financial condition. His duplicity is best seen when he realizes that Vivie will not touch her mother's tainted money. In some ways, Frank is the biggest hypocrite of all. When the source of Mrs. Warren's fortune becomes known, Frank says to Praed, "I can't marry her now" and explains, "I really cant bring myself to touch the old woman's money now"; when Praed asks him, "was that what you were going to marry on?" Frank confesses, "what else? I haven't any money, nor the smallest turn for making it."[31] In other words, Frank is himself a prostitute, looking for someone to support him for his attractiveness. As Carpenter says, Frank Gardner tries to "sell himself to Vivie," "using his good looks as bait," because "his only way to security is to become a paid husband."[32] His rejection of Mrs. Warren's tainted money is a stinging irony, for he is as much of a prostitute as she.

Frank's father, Reverend Sam, is so blatantly a sham that his pathetic efforts at honesty are merely comical. He pretends to write his own sermons but buys them instead; he does not want Kitty Warren, a whore, to come to his house but is implicated in a past affair with her; he upbraids his son for being a wastrel but cannot remember what he did in his drunkenness the night before; and he works to maintain respectability but cannot even gain the respect of his son. The essence of Sam Gardner is dramatized by means of the garden image in act 1 as he arrives at the garden gate to speak to his son. When Frank tells him to come inside, the reverend replies, "No sir; not until I know whose garden I am entering"[33] (his self-righteousness is undercut when Kitty Warren appears and he recognizes her as Mrs. Vavasour, and Kitty says, "I have a whole album of your letters still").[34] Nevertheless, Reverend Gardner knows the essential value of gardens in terms of one's reputation and social acceptability.

Sir George Crofts also insists on no pretenses. Although he is a man with a title, he does not pretend to enjoy the pleasures of his class. Even Vivie admires him "for being strong minded enough to enjoy himself in his own way [...] instead of living the usual shooting, hunting, dining-out, tailoring, loafing life of his set."[35] He thinks of himself as devoid of the lies of society: "When I say a thing I mean it; when I feel a sentiment I feel it in earnest; and what I value I pay hard money for."[36] This is the height of dissimulation and a perfect demonstration of how deception is practiced in the garden, for what he says later belies this kind of openness; in fact, because he knows all the rules and has inside knowledge of how it all works, he becomes the chief spokesperson for the system. At the climactic scene, when he and Vivie have their confrontation, the audience, as well as Vivie, learns through Sir George the truth about respectable society and the rules of the garden. First, in spite of his self-professed honesty, when the subject of Kitty Warren's profession comes up, Crofts lies when he tells Vivie that he and Kitty Warren are in the hotel business. When Vivie warns him that she already knows the truth, he reveals his intention to deceive her: "I'd never have told you."[37] After Vivie calls him a scoundrel, he defends himself by pointing to other hypocrites in polite society (the Duke of Belgravia and the archbishop of Canterbury).[38] When Vivie expresses guilt over spending her mother's money, Crofts tries to reassure her by explaining how society operates: "As long as you don't fly openly in the face of society, society doesn't ask any inconvenient questions."[39] He then articulates the cardinal principle: "There are no secrets better kept than the secrets everybody guesses."[40] Crofts implicates himself as part of that society, and this is the epiphany in the play for Vivie. When she learns that the code of the garden is to keep up a good front and never to speak the truth about what people want to hide, she flees through the garden gate.

Kitty Warren is also critical of the pretensions of society: "The hypocrisy of the world makes me sick!"[41] she says, and "I can't stand saying one thing when everyone knows I mean another. What's the use in such hypocrisy?"[42] But she is not free from hypocrisy herself. In her first private talk with her daughter, she reveals that "respectability" is the most important thing in her scale of values, using the word over and over. By conversation's end, it is clear that for Kitty Warren respectability is not based on what one does but on how well one deceives society. And it is all carried off through polite pretenses. The garden motif receives a powerful demonstration and helps to dramatize in one brief scene how it all works when Frank, who tries to calm his nervous father with "say any blessed thing except the truth," and who has just called Mrs. Warren a "wicked old devil,"[43] turns to her as she enters and stands in the garden, and, as Shaw describes it, in *"an ecstasy of dissimulation,"* says, dripping with hypocrisy, "ever so delighted to see you Mrs Warren. This quiet old rectory garden becomes you perfectly."[44] Of course the audience knows that in Kitty's mind, because of her constant references to her sister, a former prostitute who now lives next to the cathedral in Winchester ("she likes good society, and has the air of being a lady"),[45] a rectory garden is the epitome of respectability. Vivie sees through Frank's hypocrisy and scolds Frank: "You were making fun of my mother just now when you said that about the rectory garden. That is barred in future. Please treat my mother with as much respect as you treat your own."[46] Vivie wants respect for her mother, but Frank gives her respectability. The scene, with the garden as signifier, encapsulates how the hypocrisy of society functions, as well as the difference between Vivie and her mother.

This difference is brought out even more clearly in their final confrontation, which exemplifies Shaw's "drama of discussion." After each argues her own point of view and it becomes clear that Vivie intends never to see her mother again, Kitty begins to lament that she tried to make her daughter into a "good woman" and swears from this point on she will "do wrong and nothing but wrong" to her "last hour."[47] Vivie praises this declaration of honesty. "Yes: it's better to choose your line and go through with it."[48] She also clarifies that she is not judging her mother on moral grounds, even admitting that she might well have done the same thing as her mother had she been in her mother's position. Then she gives the real reason she fled from the garden earlier and is rejecting her mother now: "but I would not have lived one life and believed in another."[49] It is the practice of this convention that causes her to say, "you are a conventional woman at heart. That is why I am bidding you goodbye now."[50]

Vivie is set apart from the other characters in the play in name as well as in nature. Shaw very carefully spares her any real association with the garden-related names of the others. On the one hand, no one, not even Kitty herself, knows for sure who Vivie's father is. All that Kitty can tell her daughter is that it is none that "you have ever met. I'm sure of that, at least."[51] On the other hand, since Warren is a name assumed by her mother, it cannot be Vivie's "real" name either. All that is certain is that her name is Vivie, a name that suggests life. Indeed, Vivie does seem to embody traits of a woman in touch with her "life force," especially as she is able to defy society's dictates and live according to her own personhood.[52] Vivie wants honesty in all things, with no pretenses, no illusions, and no dreams, and she seems to live as honestly and truthfully as she can, even if it means admitting that she studied only for the money she would get, that her education has made her an "ignorant barbarian," that art and culture are boring, or that Praed, Frank, Crofts, and her own mother are all hypocrites.

Because Vivie is dissociated from the garden motif, because she is determined to be painfully truthful and realistic in all matters, and because she is contrasted with the garden-related characters, the audience gets a better understanding of the significance of the garden image. The garden functions in the play as a superficially and ironically pleasant place, under a *cloudless sky,* for social intercourse, which really means maintaining a respectable surface on everything, and, even though it is surrounded by an entrapping fence, it allows a view of freedom beyond. Vivie, repulsed by garden conduct, is the only one who can grasp for this freedom, and she flees from this garden to the city where, she hopes, honesty, hard work, and ability have a better chance to succeed. What she leaves behind, as Ganz says, is a world in which "aesthetics are irrelevant, economics are corrupt, and emotional demands intolerable."[53]

A short time before Shaw decided to take up playwriting, he said that the time was ripe "for the emergence of an extremely unpleasant and unpalatable author, one who would tackle the large number of shams, repressions, sentimentalities and insincerities and ideals of which the English was [*sic*] so proud."[54] While *Widowers' Houses* was an effective beginning of his intention of being that playwright, *Mrs. Warren's Profession* is the fulfillment of that role for himself. Significantly enough, while the garden and library help Shaw fulfill his effort in his first play, *Mrs. Warren's Profession* supplements his use of the garden, but not the library, to help him fulfill his purpose in exposing the hypocrisy that fosters the "shams, repressions, sentimentalities, and insincerities and ideals" of which the English were so proud.

3

Arms and the Man

"I Took Care to Let Them Know That We Have a Library"

While scholars have approached *Arms and the Man* with a myriad of interpretations, many agree that one of the overarching concerns of the play is the clash between romanticism and realism.[1] As Lawrence Perrine says, "the thematic conflict . . . is between realism and romantic idealism,"[2] and Charles Carpenter refines it further by pointing out that the play's purpose is to "reduce the romantic to absurdity and to preach the worth of the real."[3] Arthur Ganz specifies that "reality is represented by Bluntschli, the Swiss professional soldier, and illusion by the Bulgarians,"[4] adding that the particular ideal that Shaw sets out to denigrate is "the romantic dream of military glory."[5] Louis Crompton adds that it debunks "the quixotic notion of honor and courage," not honor and courage themselves.[6] Charles Berst's intelligent analysis admits that "romance and reality" form the battlefield of the play, while there is "no doubt as to which wins out," but he carries it a step beyond other scholars and finds the nature of the battle interesting in "its ability to reveal fully the strengths, weaknesses, and similarities of the contending qualities."[7] Berst, recognizing that Shaw rarely writes in simple black-and-white terms, views Shaw as not creating a simple romanticism-versus-realism conflict, with realism winning, but that the characters combine both qualities in themselves, expressing "the interlocking relationship and mutual dependence of romanticism and realism."[8] In sum, Berst notes that "illusions about war, gentility, and love are ultimately given their true perspective through prosaic awareness, but at the same time . . . such awareness is most vitally attached to life when it is combined with the incentive power of romance."[9] This battle of idealism and realism is carried out in the sets as well, specifically with the library and garden. Shaw, aware of the power of the performance value of appropriate settings, draws on the library and garden settings to present the romantic illusions about these settings; then he imbues these same settings with verisimilitude in order to defeat the romantic notions with its opposite. Furthermore, Shaw takes up his position on the side of realism in the physical world by using lifelike details and historical accuracy as part of the fabric of the play itself. Bernard Dukore points out that when Shaw wrote his essay "A Dramatic Realist to His Critics," he was signaling with his title his view that the play is "realistic in its depiction of character and action." [10] When Shaw learned that there were protests by Bulgarian students against his play and that it had been banned at the Burg Theatre in Austria because it was feared it "would inflame the Balkan States," [11] Shaw was delighted, or as he put it, "charmed and flattered," because he viewed the reaction as a result of the accurate depictions in his play. Samuel Weiss notes that "Shaw was enormously pleased with the censor's vindicating—so he claimed—the realism of his play." [12] Weiss points out that Shaw wrote to William Archer, "this tribute to the political actuality and ethnographical verisimilitude of my play will, I hope, be a warning to you not to disparage my historical researches in future." [13] Weiss adds that a comparison of Shaw's own sketches for the play's costumes with "Bulgarian and Serbian uniforms and Bulgarian peasant costumes reveals his painstaking accuracy." [14] The Petkoffs' library and garden help to contribute to the accuracy and authenticity of the details of Shaw's play, but ultimately go well beyond that purpose, too.

To understand the full implications of Shaw's library and garden usage, some knowledge is needed of the historical background to the play, for which Shaw did detailed research, and of the Bulgarian people he depicts. After centuries of Turkish rule, Bulgaria was liberated by Russia after it declared war against Turkey in 1877, with the final result that Bulgaria was dependent on the Russian army for protection, and the Bulgarian people were left with little cultural identity. When the czarina's nephew, Alexander of Battenberg and Prince of Bulgaria, joined an insurrection against Turkey in Eastern Rumelia in 1885, the czar withdrew the Russian general, who was the Bulgarian minister of war, and all Russian officers from the Bulgarian army. Weiss writes that Serbia, envious of Bulgaria's expansion, invaded Bulgaria on 14 November" 1885. [15] But the withdrawal of Russian officers created opportunities for junior Bulgarian officers, "who had been stymied by their Russian superiors, to advance rapidly." [16] Thus young Bulgarians became captains, and "leading Bulgarian officers were promoted to majors."[17] This explains in part the self-consciousness and insecurities of Sergius and Petkoff ("inferiority complexes, exalted patriotism, and pompous arrogance," as Roumiana Deltcheva describes it)[18] and their need to pretend to a superiority and inflated self-image, which is particularly revealed through Shaw's use of the library and garden.

The other effect of the years of Turkish occupation was on the people of Bulgaria, a population of mainly peasants. Crompton notes that "hardly any group [in Bulgaria] aspired even to middle-class manners,"[19] and Edward Dicey, a contemporary of Shaw's, described the Bulgarians as not "an engaging or particularly attractive people. . . . They are simply a race of peasants with all a peasant's meannesses and prejudices, but also with all the peasants' virtues of industry and frugality."[20] Even Shaw, in his essay "A Dramatic Realist to His Critics," acknowledges that the Bulgarians, after centuries of "miserable bondage," were "but beginning to work out their own redemption from barbarism."[21] Shaw was keenly aware of the nature of the people he was writing about, and he used the library and garden settings to capture in graphic detail the essence of that nature. A comment that might be particularly appropriate to the Petkoffs is made by Samuel Weiss when he points out that in a population "comprising mainly peasants, class barriers between the richer and poorer strata were less rigid than in more developed Western nations,"[22] even though, as he concludes, Shaw grasped the essential social changes occurring with "nascent capitalism and an increasingly important bourgeoisie in an overwhelmingly peasant nation."[23] The Petkoffs' motivation, attitude, behavior, and self-consciousness, then, is better understood when we realize that they are trying desperately to separate themselves from the peasant population and to help form an elite social class.[24]

Shaw's attack on pretentiousness and aspiration to upper-class gentility (Berst labels it a "satire on the nature of the genteel classes")[25] focuses on the Petkoff family, particularly the mother, Catherine, and the father, Major Paul Petkoff. It is true that the Petkoffs are better off than the other villagers, who are mostly peasants, and wield considerable local power. One proof of this is seen when the servant Nicola scolds the maid, Louka, for her latent insolence toward the Petkoffs: "How long would your father be left on his little farm?"[26] Dukore points to Nicola's admonishment as evidence that they "are among the most prominent members of Bulgarian society."[27] Nicola describes the mistress of the house best when he tells Louka: "She is so grand that she never dreams that any servant could dare be disrespectful to her,"[28] and Shaw tells us that Major Petkoff is *"a cheerful, excitable, insignificant, unpolished man of about 50, naturally unambitious except as to his income and his importance in local society, but just now greatly pleased with the military rank which the war has thrust on him as a man of consequence in his town."*[29] But Shaw makes it clear that both the major and his wife, in spite of all their pretenses, have not left behind their peasant roots with their plebian, uncouth, and coarse habits. In Catherine's first appearance in act 2, she *"wears a Bulgarian apron over a once brilliant but now half worn-out dressing gown, and a colored handkerchief tied over her thick black hair,* [...] *with Turkish slippers on her bare feet."*[30] Shaw underscores the incongruity by noting that she looks *"astonishingly handsome and stately under all the circumstances."*[31] Major Petkoff's real nature is revealed when he says, "all this washing cant be good for the health: it's not natural. [...] I don't mind a good wash once a week to keep up my position; but once a day is carrying the thing to a ridiculous extreme."[32]

The library motif is initiated in act 1 with the arrival of the fleeing Serbian soldier, Bluntschli. When the Petkoff daughter, Raina, tries to impress the soldier with the status of the family into whose house he has fled, she informs him, "you do not yet know in whose house you are. I am a Petkoff." "A pet what?" queries the soldier. "I mean that I belong to the family of the Petkoffs, the richest and best known in our country."[33] She tells him that her father "holds the highest command of any Bulgarian in our army. He is [*proudly*] a Major!" She lets him know that their house is a two-storied one and even has "a flight of stairs inside to get up and down by."[34] And then, in order to really impress him, she asks, "Do you know what a library is?" He replies, "A library? A roomful of books?" and she brags, "Yes. We have one, the only one in Bulgaria." Bluntschli responds, "Actually a real library! I should like to see that," and Raina explains: "I tell you these things to shew you that you are not in the house of ignorant country folk."[35] While Raina, as part of her romantic naïveté, has a sense of mystique about the library, Bluntschli, a stranger who has not been identified yet, is "the professional realist";[36] he is slightly patronizing, and he plays along with her game because at this point he is, as Raina says, "at my mercy."[37] The use of the word *library* throughout the play becomes a snobbish litany by all members of the family, using the word at every possible opportunity. We hear "he is in the library," "in full view of the library windows,"[38] "he is in the library with Major Saranoff,"[39] the "master" is "busy in the library,"[40] "is the library door shut?"[41] and "he knew quite well I was in the library."[42]

A moment of insight comes when Petkoff complains, "those stupid people of mine thought I was out here, instead of in the—haw!—library." Shaw then betrays the Petkoffs' romanticized concept of a library and reveals that Petkoff *"cannot mention the library without betraying how proud he is of it."*[43]

The library is a point of great pride—and pretense—but the illusion of a library eventually meets with the fact that the concept is a romantic mirage. Shaw, saving his ironic revelation for the climactic moment, sets act 3 *in* the library. The whole description of the room is one long sobering depiction, and the truthful facts of it mock the Petkoffs' romanticized attitude toward it. Shaw describes the scene: *"In the library after lunch. It is not much of a library. Its literary equipment consists of a single fixed shelf stocked with old paper covered novels, broken backed, coffee stained, torn and thumbed; and a couple of little hanging shelves with a few gift books on them."*[44]

Shaw adds, after pointing to the *"trophies of war and the chase"* on the wall, that *"it is a comfortable sitting room,"* perhaps implying that that is the proper nomenclature for it. Then he adds, *"there is one object, however, hopelessly out of keeping with its surroundings. This is a small kitchen table, much the worse for wear, fitted as a writing table with an old canister full of pens, an eggcup filled with ink, and a deplorable scrap of heavily used pink blotting paper."*[45] The old kitchen table, which the Petkoffs call a "desk," underscores the abyss between the cultural pretenses of the Petkoffs and their impoverished awareness. In brief, the whole concept of the "library" is a stinging parody, suggesting the extreme degree of the Petkoffs' pretentiousness, self-delusion, naïveté, and provincialism. Shaw's use of the library combines two of the poles of the play, romantic delusion and factual accuracy, and strikes at the very heart of the nature of the Petkoffs, capturing with uncanny accuracy their historical situation.

In terms of structure, it should also be noted that the whole play has been driving toward this scene in this mislabeled room that contains the climax of the play. Through the many twists and turns of the plot that occur in the library, in performance this shabby library, being the delusion that it is, would stand glaringly before the audience's eyes as the action moves toward honesty, toward the unmasking that takes place in the scene, into the light of the facts. The truth descends on the characters to displace the romantic notions that have imbued a number of the characters: Bluntschli notes that the Bulgarian officers (Sergius and Petkoff) "send for their wives to keep discipline";[46] Raina asks Bluntschli, "how did you find me out?"

when he is not convinced by her "noble attitude" and "thrilling voice";[47] Louka convinces Sergius that true courage is when someone marries the person they love in spite of their social rank;[48] Sergius observes, "everything I think is mocked by everything I do";[49] Sergius also realizes that war is a "fraud," "a hollow sham, like love" and life is a "farce,"[50] while Bluntschli points out to Raina that Sergius has "found himself out now"[51] (as she had earlier); Raina comes to understand that Sergius has been making love to Louka her maid, and so their "romance is shattered";[52] everyone discovers that Bluntschli is the chocolate cream soldier; and Catherine and Petkoff become resigned to the fact that Sergius's and Raina's engagement is off. Finally, as David Sauer notes, Raina becomes a "real person whose reactions are not feigned but her own," declaring "freedom from the role-playing she had done at the start of the play";[53] and Raina and Bluntschli become affianced. The real facts have overtaken all the romantic posturing and the library has become what it really is, "a comfortable sitting room."

The library motif also functions, in a way, in Raina's romantic idealism and her view of Sergius as a romantic hero, mainly by way of a related book motif, another component of Shaw's satire.

One of Shaw's attacks on romanticism focuses on Raina and her betrothed, Sergius Saranoff. At the beginning Raina has a starry-eyed view of romantic, idealized love, of what she calls the "higher love,"[54] which we soon learn is a heavy burden to carry. Bluntschli describes her as having an "imagination full of fairy princes and noble natures and cavalry charges and goodness knows what!"[55] Raina calls Sergius "my hero! My king!" while Sergius calls her "my queen!"[56] In addition to love, Raina talks romantically about "our heroic ideals,"[57] while both Raina and Sergius have a romantic, idealized attitude toward war as well. When Raina's mother, Catherine, describes Sergius's accomplishment in battle—"the first man to sweep through their guns"[58]—in glowing romantic terms, Raina responds, "it proves that all our ideas were real after all."[59] Sergius says, "I have gone through the war like a knight in a tournament with his lady looking down at him!"[60] By play's end, both Raina and Sergius have been disabused of their romantic idealisms, both serving Shaw's purpose.

In Shaw's description at the beginning of the scene in the library in act 3, he notes that Raina *"is gazing in a daydream out at the Balkan landscape, with a neglected novel in her lap."*[61] It is a tableau reminiscent of Blanche in *Widower's Houses* sitting in the library surrounded by expensive, leather-bound, tooled editions of the classics and reading *The Queen*. We know that the Petkoffs' "library" consists of "old paper covered novels,"[62] the popular, cheap, romantic novels of the age and likely the source of Raina's romantic idealism. Raina seems to be the only one in the family who reads them, aside from Louka, who runs "up here to the library whenever she gets a chance, to look at the books."[63] As in other plays, *Misalliance* for example, Shaw attacks not only romantic idealism but also the type of literature that spawns such attitudes.

In the opening scene of the play, Raina is specific about the source of her romantic idealism when she tells her mother that recently, when Sergius was holding her in his arms and looking into her eyes, she wondered if she had such "heroic ideas" because she is "so fond of reading Byron and Pushkin."[64] Shaw sneeringly develops the Byronic motif elsewhere. When Shaw describes Saranoff as having *"physical hardihood and high spirit,"* he points out that *"the result is precisely what the advent of nineteenth century thought first produced in England: to wit, Byronism."*[65] After a lengthy description of Saranoff, Shaw concludes by pointing out that he has the *"half tragic, half ironic air, the moodiness etc. by which Childe Harold fascinated the grandmothers of his English contemporaries."*[66] Shaw then makes the connection for us: *"It is clear that here or nowhere is Raina's ideal hero."*[67] Raina has found a real-life Byronic hero in Saranoff, based on her literary model and literary inspiration. Shaw makes an even more overt connection for us when, in act 1, as Raina climbs into bed, *"she selects a novel from the little pile of books […] and prepares to read herself to sleep. But before abandoning herself to fiction, she raises her eyes once more, thinking of the blessed reality* [Shaw's irony], *and murmurs,* My hero! My hero!"[68]

There are times in other plays when Shaw brings the library and garden motifs together, and one such scene occurs in *Arms and the Man*, when Catherine and her husband are discussing the subject of what constitutes proper conduct, introducing the tension between romantic self-images (their pretensions) and social realities (another form of delusions). Catherine, after calling him a "barbarian at heart," admonishes her husband, "I hope you behaved yourself before all those Russian officers."

PETKOFF. I did my best. I took care to let them know that we have a library.

CATHERINE. Ah; but you didn't tell them that we have an electric bell in it? I have had one put up.

PETKOFF. What's an electric bell?

CATHERINE. You touch a button [...] and then Nicola comes up.
PETKOFF. Why not shout for him?[69]

Catherine informs her husband that "civilized people never shout for their servants. I've learnt that while you were away."[70] Petkoff, defending himself, retorts, "well, I'll tell you something I've learnt too. Civilized people don't hang out their washing to dry [on the bushes in the garden] where visitors can see it." Catherine responds, "I don't believe really refined people notice such things."[71] When a couple have a "debate" over what constitutes refinement, the implication is that neither of them knows very much about the subject, thus dramatizing Shaw's biting irony by using both the library and garden to expose the real truth underneath their romantic self-conceptions.

Act 2 takes place in the Petkoffs' garden, and Shaw describes it in meticulous detail: *"In the garden of Major Petkoff's house. It is a fine spring morning: the garden looks fresh and pretty."*[72] As in so many of Shaw's garden settings, the surface appearance is very pleasant and attractive—and it is another fine morning—while underneath the implications are darker and more devastating. Shaw adds, *"Beyond the paling the tops of a couple of minarets can be seen shewing that there is a valley there, with the town in it."*[73] This detail indicates that, while the town sits in a valley and that we can see the tops of several minarets from their garden, the Petkoff house sits above the rest of the village. In performance, this view would be a strong and constant reminder of how the Petkoffs see themselves, lofty and superior to all the rest of the Bulgarians, visually, figuratively, and literally. Shaw continues, *"A few miles further the Balkan mountains rise and shut in the landscape."*[74] The fact that the Petkoffs and their little village are "shut in" by the large mountains suggests their relationship to the world at large, from which they are closed off, isolated, and limited. Again, in performance the audience would sense the claustrophobia created by the imposing mountains, and the provincial attitude of the Petkoffs is illuminated by the geography. Shaw continues his description: *"On the right the stable yard, with its gateway, encroaches on the garden. There are fruit bushes along the paling and house, covered with washing spread out to dry."*[75] Weiss reminds us that the rising bourgeoisie Bulgarians had within their walls "lush gardens."[76] While the possession of a garden may signify gentility, civilized discourse, and upper-class status, especially in a country such as England, this clearly is not "that" kind of garden. Like the library, it is not much of a garden, certainly not of the upper-class, social-interchange kind. The stable yard's intrusion into the garden suggests that this is a garden with a practical purpose; similarly, the clothes spread out to dry on the bushes also suggests a practical role for the "garden." What Shaw suggests is that these people are, at heart, peasant folk, practical, simple, and provincial, living in a workaday world. This reality stands in stark contrast to their obvious social pretensions, their status-seeking, their desire for "civilized" behavior, their need for respectability, and their blatant hypocrisy and fraudulent self-image. Their garden is as much a piece of devastating irony as the library is.

The garden scene is important in other ways as well. It is in the garden in act 2 that Major Sergius Saranoff first makes his appearance in the play, and the stable yard and the clothes drying on the fruit bushes provide a realistic counterpoint to Saranoff's facade of the knightly, cavalier, romantic hero. In fact, Charles Berst points out that the "romantic, Byronic Sergius," "is in contrast with the laundry on the fruit bushes and the after-breakfast atmosphere."[77] Moreover, the garden scene contains a major turning point in the play's movement from romantic balderdash to plain facts. When Raina enters, she and Sergius exchange their nauseating illusions about "my hero! My king," "my queen, "a knight in a tournament" and the "higher love."[78] No sooner does Raina exit the scene than Sergius turns to Louka, the maid, and complains about how fatiguing it is "to keep up for any length of time" the "higher love."[79] Then he begins to attempt to make love to the maid and recognizes, in a striking moment of self-honesty, what a "buffoon," "humbug," and "blackguard" he is.[80] Louka also informs Sergius that Raina has another man in her life and rubs truth in Sergius's face: "I know the difference between the sort of manner you and she put on before one another and the real manner."[81] And when Raina tells her mother a little later, "I sometimes wish you could marry him [Sergius] instead of me,"[82] the audience realizes the truth of the situation, and all the romantic illusions that had motivated Sergius and Raina are belied and symbolized by the real-world commonness of the stable door and the laundry on the bushes in an "aristocratic" garden.

The action in this garden also underscores the hypocrisy. It is here that Sergius and Raina talk of their "higher love," after which Sergius begins making love to the maid, Louka, who tells Sergius that Raina is doing the same thing behind his back,[83] and Catherine tries mightily to hide the fact that Bluntschli was the Serbian soldier in Raina's room at the beginning of the play. Shaw uses the garden setting effectively once again to reveal the truth hiding beneath the surface of the would-be middle class.

Thus, in *Arms and the Man* Shaw again uses the library and the garden settings in highly significant and meaningful ways. The garden setting contains the major turning point in the antiromantic/idealism theme, which involves the falsity of Sergius's and Raina's romantic pretensions, while the library completes the journey from romantic delusion into the glaring light of the factual world.

4

Candida

A Wall of Bookshelves and the Best View of the Garden

Of all of Shaw's earlier plays, it is perhaps with *Candida* that gardens and libraries contribute the most to understanding some of the deeper nuances and implications of Shaw's intentions in certain aspects of the play.

Much of the scholarship on the play shows that *Candida* is a challenging play with widely divergent and contradictory opinions about it. As Arthur Ganz writes, *Candida* is "one of the richest, most attractive, and most elusive of Shaw's earlier plays,"[1] even though James Woodfield says that Morell and Marchbanks are "relatively transparent and easily understood" and "contain little mystery."[2] Walter King concludes that there "remains a considerable puzzle, even to critics sympathetic to Shavian ideology and esthetic."[3] Arthur Nethercot sums it up, observing, "for years critic after critic, reader after reader, spectator after spectator have interpreted Candida, Morell, and Marchbanks according to their own temperaments and predilections" and that the work "still remains a mystery."[4] While a study of the functioning of gardens and libraries in *Candida* may not solve all the puzzles of the play, they do at least cast a somewhat clearer light on one character, and that is Morell.

A few examples will illustrate the challenges and diversity of opinions about the play. Charles Berst says that the central element of the play is the "love relationship to Candida"[5] by Morell and Marchbanks and the object of the play is to "explore and open up three diverse views of reality"[6] while the "real action of the play derives from the major characters asserting different attitudes toward life . . . rising out of their most basic psychological promptings and estimates of reality";[7] Woodfield contends that Shaw's "immediate target is marriage" and "the roles of the partners and the nature of women"[8] while also stressing the "religious context" of the play;[9] Walter Lazenby argues that the changes in the characters "exemplify the twin Shavian themes that getting rid of illusions is healthy and that the individual must resist system to be vital";[10] Jacob Adler says that the "motivating force of the play" is Marchbanks's desire for "truth," which is "no help to the marriage";[11] William Doan contends that *Candida* is a play "founded on the power of the eye";[12] and, while speculating that the possibility that "somewhere there exists a key for [*Candida's*] interpretation," King asserts that "if there be one, it lies within the rhetoric of the play."[13]

While differences of opinion about the main concerns of *Candida* are numerous, an even greater divergence of opinion exists about the characters themselves, and while much of the discussion revolves around the characters of Candida and Marchbanks, a virtual morass of opposing views exists for Morell. Additionally, any study of the setting of *Candida* forces the attention on Morell, because it is his world the play inhabits, and it warrants a closer examination.

On the one hand, staunch supporters of Morell, such as Charles Berst, defend the minister, even in the face of his apparent weaknesses, such as his pomposity. Berst warns that "the actor who plays up Morell's pomposity and thick-headedness will be missing the full reverberations and strength of his character"[14] and defends his preachiness by pointing out that Morell is a "man in whom rhetoric and feeling coalesce."[15] Berst goes on to add that Morell's praise of Marchbanks "captures the inherent kindliness of Morell"[16] and blames Candida for not appreciating "the strengths of [Morell's] character."[17] Elsie Adams argues that Morell's being the weaker of the two and in greater need of Candida's love "does not imply that Shaw meant him to be contemptible" and goes so far as to suggest that Morell is "the sort of man Shaw liked and, in many ways, the sort of man Shaw was."[18]

On the other hand, Morell has his detractors. Charles Carpenter asserts that Morell's delusion that his "practiced rhetoric is capable of meeting any challenge, evokes derisive and at times contemptuous laughter,"[19] and Harold Pagliaro believes that if one accepts what Candida says about Morell's lifelong dependency on women, then he "is reduced to a nullity, except as the sire of her children."[20] John Lucas theorizes that Morell had "been heading for a fall, and we enjoy his discomfiture, the deflating of his male ego,"[21] while Patrick White points out that his father-in-law, Burgess, "thinks him a fool."[22] Herbert Bergman, reflecting Marchbanks's point of view, adds that Morell's "metaphors, sermons [and] stale perorations are mechanical, artificial, and empty, revealing neither 'reality, truth [nor] freedom.'"[23]

There are also balanced accounts of him, starting with those of Shaw himself, whose position seems a little more fair. In a letter to Arnold Daly, who was playing Marchbanks with great success in New York in 1903–1904, Shaw labels Morell "a conceited fool" on the one hand and on the other hand calls him a "really good and able man."[24] Others have followed Shaw's cautious lead. Lazenby says that Morell "has been not a buffoonish caricature of weakness but a subtle mixture of weaknesses and strengths,"[25] while Pagliaro points out that "we may see Morell . . . as an overly indulged windbag, utterly dependent on his wife—when in fact he has won the remarkable Candida's love to begin with."[26]

The setting of *Candida*, in spite of the title of the play, clearly belongs to Reverend James Mavor Morell. It is not the kitchen, the scullery, the world of paraffin lamps and slicing onions, nor the world of the nursery or the bedroom, all domains that belong to Candida (as Virginia Woolf reminds us in *A Room of One's Own*, women's rooms are the kitchen, the nursery, and the bedroom). The world of the play belongs to Morell, the offstage settings being the parish he serves and the parsonage (their habitat by virtue of his position as parish priest), and, onstage, his library. Shaw's use of a part of London, Victoria Park, and its implications, as well as the onstage setting, Morell's library, which is an extension of the offstage setting, clearly point to and help define Morell.

In the opening stage descriptions, Shaw gives us three pages of highly detailed, almost poetical, description, an indicator, knowing Shaw's habits, that extremely close scrutiny must be given to what he has meticulously described for the reader. It is important because Shaw makes it important. Another curious feature is that he gives one entire page to describing the offstage world that the audience does not get a single glimpse of. What is Shaw's purpose in describing at great length a setting that only a reader knows about? It is a question to be considered.

We note in the first sentence that, as is so often the case with Shaw, it is *"A fine morning* [. . . and] *the sun is shining cheerfully; there is no fog."*[27] Shaw's predilection for *"fine"* weather is operative again, but in this case, the implication is that Morell, at least at the beginning of the play, is in his heaven, all is right with his world, in his "kingdom of Heaven on earth."

The area in which the play takes place is *"in the north east quarter of London, a vast district miles away from the London of Mayfair and St James's, and much less narrow, squalid, fetid and airless in its slums. It is strong in unfashionable middle class life."*[28] In other words, it is the working-class area of the East End, the seedbed of socialist thought. Shaw also notes that along the *"main thoroughfares"* there exists the *"luxury of grass-grown 'front gardens' untrodden by the foot of man save as to the path from the gate to the hall doors.*[29] These small patches of grass serve as a contrast to Morell's garden settings. Shaw also emphasizes the fact that it is composed of *"endured monotony of miles and miles of unlovely brick houses"* and nothing seems able *"to break the monotony."*[30] Amid all this bleakness stands the parsonage of St. Dominic, obviously unlike and in contrast to the working-class world around it. *"This desert of unattractiveness,"* as Shaw calls it, has as an oasis, *"a park of 217 acres, fenced in, not by railings, but by a wooden paling, and containing plenty of greensward, trees, a lake for bathers, flower beds which are triumphs of the admired cockney art of carpet gardening, and a sandpit [. . .]. Wherever the prospect is bounded by trees or rising green grounds, it is a pleasant place."*[31] Very much to the point is the fact that during the later part of the nineteenth century, this area, named Victoria Park, was largely patronized by the working classes of the East End, Morell's parishioners, and for many of their children it provided what might have been their only encounter with anything resembling a natural landscape.

Shaw also points out that where the ground stretches flat *"to the grey palings, with bricks and mortar, sky signs, crowded chimneys and smoke beyond, the prospect makes it desolate and sordid."*[32] Several things are of note here. At one end of the park commanding the *"best view of Victoria Park,"*[33] abutting the park, sits St. Dominic's parsonage, the abode of the Reverend James Mavor Morell. It is as though this vast, lovely piece of nature in the middle of a large area of squalor is Morell's own personal garden, for, as Shaw points out, the best view of it all is from the "glass window" in Morell's study before which his chair sits. Shaw also notes that the garden is enclosed, not by a railing, which anyone would be able to climb over, but by a *"paling,"*[34] obviously tall enough to force people to enter only at the gates, thereby limiting the amount of traffic pathways into the park. Whereas in *Mrs. Warren's Profession* the paling is designed to keep people, such as Vivie, in, this paling's purpose is to keep people out. We note also that the park closes at nighttime (its current daily hours are from 7 a.m. to dusk), for when Marchbanks threatens to take a walk in the park in act

3, Candida responds, "nonsense: it's closed long ago,"[35] making it even less busy for Morell's enjoyment in the evenings. We know also that while the skyline all around the park is dotted with *"bricks and mortar, sky signs, crowded chimneys and smoke beyond,"* from St. Dominic's parsonage, *"not a brick is visible."*[36] Finally, Shaw also points out that the parsonage, *"semi-detached,"* has a *"front garden and a porch."*[37] In other words, while others in his neighborhood must content themselves with one little patch of lawn as their garden, Morell has *two* gardens, one consisting of a 217-acre park, and one in front of his porch.

There is another way Victoria Park is relevant to Morell. In addition to being one of the best East End parks, it also came to be known as "the People's Park" for its being a popular place for political meetings, speakers, and rallies. It is located in the Tower Hamlets borough; Hackney, with its long tradition of religious dissent and non-conformism, abuts it to the north. Tower Hamlets is the core of the "East End," an area which, by the nineteenth century, was notoriously overcrowded with poor people and immigrants. The East End had attracted the attention of social reformers as early as the eighteenth century, and Tower Hamlets became known for its leftist politics, including communism. The radicalism of the East End contributed to the formation of the Labour Party. Morell's social message, therefore, would be a part of the very fabric of such an area.

Victoria Park's numerous speaker's corners, where socialists such as William Morris and Annie Besant expounded on their ideas for improving the lives of the downtrodden, commonly drew large crowds. Orators spoke on a wide variety of religious, scientific, and political topics, and often several speakers lecturing at the same time, each with his own audience, scattered throughout the park. Morell's being an expounder of socialist ideas clearly coincides with this environment; indeed, it may be a necessary part of survival in such an environment.

Shaw describes Morell as *"a Christian Socialist clergyman of the Church of England, and an active member of the Guild of St Matthew and the Christian Social Union."*[38] The Guild of St. Matthew was sometimes referred to as the "shock troops" of Christian Socialism and published *The Church Reformer,* which Morell is reading in the opening scene, a Christian Socialist journal from 1845 to 1895 under the editorship of Stewart Headlam, who incidentally founded the Guild of St. Matthew and, as an ordained Anglican priest, attacked in his sermons the wide gap between rich and poor and presented Jesus Christ as a revolutionary.[39] The Christian Social Union was an organization within the Church of England devoted to the study of social conditions and the remedying of social injustice, a ministry that appealed strongly to what many called "slum priests," a label that could also describe Morell.

Shaw goes on to describe Morell physically as *"a vigorous, genial, popular man of forty, robust and goodlooking, full of energy, with pleasant, hearty, considerate manners, and a sound unaffected voice, which he uses with a wide range and perfect command of expression. He is a first rate clergyman* [. . .]. *Withal, a great baby, pardonably vain of his powers and unconsciously pleased with himself."*[40] But Shaw's overt description of Morell is supplemented and given added definition by the nuances suggested by means of Shaw's use of an urban London setting.

When Shaw comes to describing the onstage setting, he adds more dimensions to Morell's character. The first thing he points out is that the drawing room, as Shaw calls it but which is in fact Morell's space and a library, has a *"large plate glass window looking out on the park."*[41] Furthermore, when the scene opens, Morell is sitting in *his* chair at *his* table, from which, according to Shaw, he *"can cheer himself with a view of the park over his left shoulder."*[42] In all this vast area of monotony and squalor, only one person has "the best view," in Shaw's words, of this 217-acre park. Furthermore, Morell is not to be disturbed; there are two outside flights of stairs, one leading up to Morell's study, the other going down to the basement; this staircase is used by *"tradesmen and members of the family."*[43] Another significant touch is that Morell sits in a *"strong round backed revolving chair"* so that he can easily turn to look out at the park whenever he wishes, and his work space is a *"long table,"*[44] obviously the largest piece of furniture in the room. By contrast, Miss Proserpine Garnett, his typist, sits at a *"little table only half as wide as the other,"* and she sits *"with her back to the window."*[45]

When Shaw describes the *"varnished wooden mantelpiece, with neatly moulded shelves,"* he notes that there are *"tiny bits of mirror let into the panels,"*[46] the idea of the mirrors suggesting narcissism, and while the stage directions have only Miss Prossy looking at herself in them (*"putting her hair straight at a panel of mirror in the mantelpiece"*[47]), the implication being that the mirrors are large enough for one to see one's face in them, and Shaw's stage directions do send Morell to the hearth a number of times.

In addition, inside "his room," Morell, according to Shaw, is *"spared from the children"* and the family meals so that he can do his work.[48] It is his private kingdom, his room, his study, his library, and his enormous park and garden, and he, and his ego, sit at the center of everything.[49]

The interior of Morell's library reflects the exterior world of Victoria Park and Tower Hamlets. Shaw tells us that *"the wall behind him* [Morell] *is fitted with bookshelves, on which an adept eye can measure the parson's casuistry and divinity by Maurice's Theological Essays and a complete set of Browning's poems, and the reformer's politics by a yellow backed Progress and Poverty, Fabian Essays, A Dream of John Ball, Marx's Capital, and half a dozen other literary landmarks in Socialism."*[50]

Of course a bookshelf is a reflection of its owner's intellectual propensities, and, in this case, of East End London and late Victorian England's interest in socialism at the time. Morell's bookshelf is in concord with the borough in which he lives and with some portion of the population of the age. Reverend Frederick Denison Maurice first published his collection of essays in 1854 followed by a number of reissues, the one in 1871 being dedicated to Alfred Lord Tennyson. Maurice's writings were foundational to the Christian Social Union; his theological position appealed to the liberal wing of the English church and obviously is admired by Morell. A copy of Browning's poetry on Morell's bookshelf may be a bit of irony on Shaw's part, for Browning, in his dramatic monologues, was one of the most astute portrayers of the human psyche, of the human ego, and especially of egomania, wherein Morell may well be able to see himself were he so inclined. Browning is also noted for his positive, optimistic, often sunny outlook on the world ("God's in his heaven, all's right with the world"), which would certainly harmonize with Morell's positive, enthusiastic temperament. The fact that Henry George's *Progress and Poverty* is *"yellow backed"* seems to suggest that its owner has read it over and over, which coincides with the phenomenon that it was the most widely read book of the time, only the Bible outselling it. George theorized that poverty is caused by everything being overtaxed, that land is common property, and all that is needed is a single tax on land, with all other taxes being abolished. Shaw himself confessed that George awakened his social conscience and changed his way of looking at the prevailing socioeconomic structure. The book's presence in the scene lets us know that Morell is in the vanguard of current, liberal thought. *A Dream of John Ball* is William Morris's fictional account of the English Peasant's Revolt in 1381. Morris, a man very much of his own time, viewed the medieval world as a brief golden age, because the peasants were prosperous and happy and protected by guilds, and the workers expressed themselves because they, through their crafts, each created complete, individual, and self-expressive artistic products in contrast to the cheap, monotonous products of the unfulfilled workers of the modern assembly lines. And Marx's *Capital* stands as a monument to socialist thought.

On the surface of it, Morell's library of *"literary landmarks in Socialism,"*[51] including the Fabian Society publication, appears to be a collection with whose owner Shaw would feel a great deal of sympathy and comradeship.[52] The real question regards Morell's underlying motivation for his socialistic leanings. We do not know if the Reverend Morell has turned to socialism because of his residence in Tower Hamlets amid crushing poverty, or whether he requested such an assignment because of his socialism. Either way, his economic beliefs fit comfortably with his East End environment, enhance his popularity, and benefit him by feeding his ego and, perhaps, slightly augmenting his bank account. The library reflects the political and social views of most of the inhabitants of Tower Hamlets, and, as for Morell's motives, we shall give him the benefit of a doubt.

Reverend Morell is an extremely popular preacher and a speaker in great demand. The opening tableau and the first business of the play—both dramatically emphatic positions—reveal Morell and his secretary, Proserpine, trying to find a place in his busy schedule for yet another speaking engagement, with his calendar reflecting the far-reaching popularity of progressive thought in some quarters of London. As he silently opens his last letter, he lets out a *"comic groan of despair,"* and the first words of the play come from Proserpine: "Another lecture?"[53] "The Hoxton Freedom Group want me to address them on Sunday morning," Morell says, and then asks, "What are they?" "Communist anarchists," replies Proserpine. "Just like Anarchists not to know that they cant have a parson on Sunday," comments Morell, who nevertheless becomes intent on accommodating them. As he asks about certain days of the week, Proserpine rattles off what amounts to a brief tour of London and finally makes it clear that he has no time for the anarchists: *"Guild of St Matthew on Monday. Independent Labor Party, Greenwich Branch, on Thursday. Monday, Social-Democratic Federation, Mile End Branch."*[54]

Shaw even pokes a little fun at himself and his own group. When Morell asks about "the 25th," Proserpine tells him that it is already taken by the Fabian Society. "Bother the Fabian Society,"[55] says Morell, perhaps revealing a slight disdain for such a group. One wonders if Shaw is suggesting that the Fabian Society is more committed to socialism than Morell is, or that the members of the Fabian Society are not idealists like himself, or that Morell is not completely sincere in his espousal of socialism. What is behind his comment, "bother the Fabian Society"? At any rate, Morell shows a certain amount of disdain for Shaw's beloved Fabians.

The point of the whole dialogue is Morell's popularity with those groups with a progressive, socialistic bent and the congruence between the interior of Morell's study and the exterior neighborhood. In the scene, it is clear that even though he is in great demand, he tries to accommodate all of them, because he does not want to pass up an opportunity to be gazed upon by audiences full of admiring people listening to his every word and adoring him. The subtlety in Morell's character becomes clearer: He delights in all the attention he gets, he luxuriates in his popularity, and his ego feeds on being in the center of his public's eye. His wife, Candida, who understands him better than anyone, confronts him with the truth about himself and his preaching: "Besides, James dear, you preach so splendidly that it's as good as a play for them. Why do you think the women are so enthusiastic?"[56] He pretends to be shocked, but she continues, "you think it's your Socialism and your religion; but if it were that, they'd do what you tell them instead of only coming to look at you"; "They're all in love with you. And you are in love with preaching because you do it so beautifully. And you think it's all enthusiasm for the kingdom of Heaven on earth; and so do they. You dear silly!"[57] She concludes with a revelatory remark, telling him, "you're spoiled with love and worship: you get far more than is good for you."[58]

Morell's message, based in large part on the books in his library, is at one with his neighborhood and, to a degree, certain other parts of London. With his parish located in a vast, socioeconomically depressed neighborhood, the logical message for him to preach is one that appeals to the people from this working-class area, and that message is socialism. It would be hard to imagine that he would have that kind of popularity if he were espousing capitalism and defending the British class system. Morell may think that he is sincere in what he does—and no doubt he is—but he can still be unaware of his underlying motivations. But Candida and Marchbanks are more objective and critical. Marchbanks grows weary of Morell's "words! words! words!" and calls him "you fool! you fool! you triple fool"[59] (of course Marchbanks's attitude has to be contextualized by the fact that he sees Morell as a rival lover), and Candida says later that Eugene "is always right."[60] As Candida and Morell engage in a frank discussion of their relationship, their feelings, and Eugene's place in it all at the end of act 2, Candida realizes "how stupid he is, and she is a little disappointed" and tells him "how little you understand me," calling his sermons "mere phrases that you cheat yourself and others with every day." Candida compares him to Eugene, the poet, who understands everything (from Candida's perspective), and she tells Morell, quite bluntly, "you, darling, you understand nothing."[61] An even more damning statement, in Shaw's hierarchy of values, comes from his wife when she tells him, "How conventional all you unconventional people are!"[62] In a condescending way, she says at one point, "My *boy* [emphasis added] shall not be worried: I will protect him,"[63] the implication being, from Candida's point of view, that he needs to be protected. In the final scene with Candida, Morel, and Marchbanks, Candida says, "James is master here,"[64] and later, when Morell cannot tell her why that is so, she explains, "I make him master here, though he does not know it, and could not tell you a moment ago how it came to be so."[65] When Candida is asked to choose between Morell and Marchbanks, she chooses Morell over Marchbanks, because, as she announces, "I give myself to the weaker of the two."[66] The whole play moves toward this resolution of conflicts by underscoring that Morell has more limitations than Marchbanks.

There may, perhaps, also be another reason for Morell's progressive, socialist message. In his stage directions, Shaw points out that *"there is nothing useless or pretentious in* [Morell's] *room, money being too scarce in the house of an east end parson to be wasted on snobbish trimmings."*[67] Morell supplements his parson's salary with his lectures, and the more he lectures the more money he makes. We know also that he is paid by means of passing a collection plate, and the more he assuages the misery of his impoverished London audiences with the message of socialistic hope, it would seem that the fuller the collection plate becomes. We know this because in act 3, when Candida asks her husband, "did you speak well?" he answers her by saying, "I have never spoken better in my life." She responds in her very next question to him after his entrance: "How much was the collection?" to which he replies, "I forgot to ask." She then turns to Eugene and says, "He must have spoken splendidly, or he would never have forgotten that."[68] This brief interchange tells us several things. First, it is the practice at his meetings to pass the collection plate (we can only assume that the procedure is the same every night); second, he is in love with his own preaching; and third, that the amount of money he collects is important to him ("he would never have forgotten that"). It may be argued that the collected money could go to the organization to whom he is speaking, but we do not know that for a fact; if the audience to whom he is speaking is composed of the group who is sponsoring him, why could they not just contribute directly to their cause, and forgo the lecture? Also, why is it so important to him, according to his wife, how much money is collected if there were not some personal benefit in it for him, and, in the same vein, why would his wife, perhaps in charge of the household budget, be so interested in knowing "how much was the collection"? It seems only logical that they would have to pay a guest speaker something, though perhaps not the entire collection. Another clue to this issue is given at the beginning of the play, when Miss Prossy is helping Morell find a place in his schedule for the Hoxton Freedom Group, and she points out, "theyre only half a dozen ignorant and conceited costermongers without five shillings between them," which implies that they are not worth his time because the collection plate would be rather empty. The socialist message in this deprived environment may be of some financial benefit, and Morell is certainly fully booked.

Experience teaches us that Shaw is an extremely thorough dramatist and that everything he puts into a play has a reason for being there. In *Candida,* Shaw uses Victoria Park as Morell's garden, and Morell's library serves as an extension of the reverend himself, giving us an insight into an important element that is an essential part of James Mavor Morell. He also captures, to a degree, late nineteenth-century Victorian London and the popularity, among that segment of the population wanting Morell's services as a lecturer, of progressive and socialist thought.

5

Man and Superman

Books on a Garden Table

Shaw's *Man and Superman* begins in a library in London and ends in a garden in Granada. This contrast in settings suggests the movement of the play, both physically (going from England to Spain) and thematically. The opening of the play focuses on Roebuck Ramsden, whose library it is; the close of the play focuses on John Tanner, whose symbolic habitat the garden is, representing nature. The play moves from Roebuck Ramsden to John Tanner. The library helps to define Ramsden, and the garden helps to define Tanner. Jack Tanner is the central character of the play; as Tanner's adversary, Roebuck Ramsden helps to define Tanner—and Tanner helps to define Ramsden. Ramsden and Tanner contrast with each other, the library and garden settings underscoring deeper and specific significances in the contrast. In no other play has Shaw so studiously drawn upon the garden and the library to fulfill his purpose.

Libraries and Books

Shaw, as usual, provides minute details in the stage descriptions of the opening scene. As usual also with Shaw, every detail has a significance. Shaw describes the scene, Ramsden's study, as a *"study, handsomely and solidly furnished* [which] *proclaims the man of means."*[1] Roebuck Ramsden prides himself on his progressiveness. Shaw notes that he *"was a Unitarian and Free Trader from his boyhood,"* an evolutionist since the publication of the *Origin of Species,* and thinks of himself as *"an advanced thinker and fearlessly outspoken reformer."*[2] In his library, against the inner wall, stands *"a stately bookcase."*[3]

Against the wall opposite him [Ramsden] *are two busts on pillars: one, to his left, of John Bright; the other, to his right, of Mr. Herbert Spencer. Between them hang an engraved portrait of Richard Cobden; enlarged photographs of Martineau, Huxley, and George Eliot; autotypes of allegories by Mr. G. F. Watts (for Roebuck believes in the fine arts with all the earnestness of a man who does not understand them), and an impression of Dupont's engraving of Delaroche's Beaux Arts hemicycle, representing the great men of all ages.*[4]

Shaw takes great pains with this very specific description, and every object in Ramsden's library belies Ramsden's view of himself.[5] While Ramsden classifies himself as an advanced thinker and fearlessly outspoken reformer, limitations in Ramsden's commitment to progressiveness exist, and while all the images in his library appear, on the surface, to be of advanced thinkers, reformers, and artists, Shaw has carefully chosen personages about whom their commitment to complete reform, or their artistic ability, is questionable.[6]

Ramsden's library is *his* space, which is, as Jung says, an extension of the self, and the nuances in Ramsden's own intellectual composition are reflected in the decor of his library. Shaw, personally, was less than happy with those who espoused progressive positions but who in reality were confused about what progressiveness was (as seen also in the Reverend James Morell in *Candida*), and he was not averse to letting his feelings about such people be known. In looking more closely at Bright, Spencer, Cobden, Martineau, Huxley, Eliot, Watts, Dupont, and Delaroche, one senses that Shaw is laughing at how Ramsden has fallen behind in his thinking and reading as revealed by the portraits and busts in Ramsden's library. And the ambiguity in the characters depicted in his study symbolizes the dichotomy in Ramsden.

While John Bright (1811–1889), one of the leading members of the Anti–Corn Law League formed in 1839 to protect factory workers from high agricultural prices, was a member of the Peace Society, denounced the Crimean War (1854–1856), and was supported by those for universal suffrage, another side of Bright's thought was not so progressive: He opposed factory legislation, trade unions, social reform, and Gladstone's Home Rule policy for Ireland,[7] a likely sore point with Shaw. The other statue in Ramsden's library, Herbert Spenser (1820–1903), a renowned political philosopher who believed in a Lamarckian evolutionary theory, defended individual liberties, advocated empiricism, and supported the "law of equal freedom," a position that led him to a belief in laissez-faire. But, again, while Spencer would be a hero for progressives, he would not be for socialists such as Shaw. While in his early days he defended a number of radical causes, such as land nationalization and the role of women in society, Spencer abandoned these later in his life. Moreover, he felt that "education, religion, the economy, and care for the sick or indigent were not to be undertaken by the state,"[8] positions which would not fit well with Shaw's socialism.

Between the two busts in Ramsden's study hang images of a number of personages from nineteenth-century British culture. The first engraved portrait that Shaw mentions is of Richard Cobden (1804–1865), a nineteenth-century cloth manufacturer who devoted much of his life to public service and worthy causes, who joined with a group of philosophic radicals, (one of whose name was *Roebuck*), and who formed the famous Anti–Corn Law League. He also worked for free trade and fought for British nonintervention in the internal affairs of other nations, he opposed a number of wars, and, as a successful manufacturer who championed causes in the name of self-interest (and that of other British manufacturers), he fought for the repeal of the corn laws for the purpose of providing cheap food for factory workers and for stimulating demand for British manufactured goods. Cobden also opposed factory legislation that would regulate the hours of labor, arguing that workmen were strong enough to protect themselves.[9] And that was liberalism at the end of the nineteenth century.

Harriet Martineau (1802–1876) was a prolific writer whose primary causes, in addition to social reform under the influence of Jeremy Bentham and John Stuart Mill, were the employment of women, state education for girls, the admission of women into the medical profession, and the right of women to vote. Certainly Shaw would empathize with such enlightened views, but two of her best-known publications were religious books such as *Devotional Exercises for the Use of Young Persons* and *Addresses, Prayers, and Hymns*.[10] Moreover, "her knowledge of economics was superficial, impressionistic, and often ill digested" and "she was aware that she was merely the popularizer of other people's ideas."[11] John Stuart Mill called her a "mere tyro."[12] Thus, as a popularizer, she could be seen as an exploiter of progressive causes for her own purposes.

While Thomas Henry Huxley (1825–1895) started out in life as a medical doctor and surgeon, he devoted his attention increasingly to biology and evolution, taking Darwin's ideas beyond Darwin and tackling the issue of the ancestry of man. His chief work on evolution, *Evidence as to Man's Place in Nature,* was short and popular in style, much like his earlier writing in popular science magazines. Near the end of his career, he was appointed to the Privy Council, where he finally became part of "the establishment," which he had always longed for,[13] an irony that would not have escaped Shaw. Moreover, Huxley was an apologist for "Social Darwinism," which Shaw attacked as "anti-social."

George Eliot (née Mary Anne Evans, 1819–1880) flaunted Victorian convention by living with George Henry Lewes as man and wife. For such a violation of Victorian codes, she was alienated from much of British society, for which, according to Lewes, she often suffered from depression over the social ridicule she felt. For her to defy society, Shaw undoubtedly would have admired her; for her to suffer guilt over it would only meet with Shaw's disdain. She was alienated from her family because of the conduct of her private life, but "her siblings probably would have been surprised to know *how conservative* [emphasis added] Mary Anne had become" by the late 1860s.[14]

Several more pictorial representations hang on Roebuck Ramsden's walls. One group consists of *"autotypes of allegories by Mr. G. F. Watts,"* a "visionary who tackled the great moral issues of his time";[15] he was an allegorist and a symbolist who eschewed realistic depictions, a style which may be beyond Ramsden's comprehension, for, as Shaw sarcastically notes, *"Roebuck believes in the fine arts with all the earnestness of a man who does not understand them."*[16] Watts's personal life, however, was not as liberated as his artistic vision. His desire to save the innocent led him into a "disastrous" marriage, at the age of forty-six, with Ellen Terry, only sixteen at the time, whom he intended to rescue from "the temptation and abominations of the stage."[17] By the time Shaw wrote *Man and Superman,* he was already in a "relationship" with Miss Terry, and one can only surmise what Shaw thought of Watts's noble effort to "save" her from the clutches of the likes of himself.

Hippolyte (Paul) Delaroche (1797–1856) was a popular illustrator who had a knack for choosing historical scenes as his subject, which appealed to the taste of the middle class, and he had a skill which attracted the public attention. While retaining public approval, he was aware of the contempt of his fellow artists for whom he would forever remain in their eyes a Philistine artist. His one piece of good fortune was that his paintings drew attention by being copied by engravers, and Henriquel-Dupont, to whom Shaw refers in his stage directions, was the best known of Delaroche's engravers. Delaroche was commissioned in the 1830s to decorate the hemicycle of the École des Beaux-Arts, which he completed in 1841, and this work, hanging in Ramsden's study, was for some time regarded as "a masterpiece of decorative painting."[18] Ramsden, who shows his Philistine taste and his perceptual limitations and who does not know good art from bad, has in his library only popularized decorative pieces.

A study of the decor in Ramsden's library leads to an understanding of Ramsden's contrast with Tanner. At issue in the opening act of *Man and Superman* is the guardianship of Ann Whitefield, whose father has left Ramsden and Tanner as joint guardians in his will. The differences between the two men provide the essential conflict of the first act and help Shaw refine and clarify his conception of a superman: having enlightened views, such as Ramsden's, is insufficient to be a superior person; going against conventional thought, such as Tanner does, provides a beginning for the necessary independence to becoming one's true self, in touch with the Life Force within. The library, as the physical extension of the content of Ramsden's and Tanner's conversation, lends an appropriate backdrop to their confrontation, for the discussion, which delineates the differences between them, centers for the most part around the debate over a book.

In the opening scene with Octavius, Ramsden picks up from the table a book, *"bound in red cloth,"* which he takes great exception to: "I have in my hand a copy of the most infamous, the most scandalous, the most mischievous, the most blackguardly book that ever escaped burning at the hands of the common hangman."[19] Ramsden then admits that he has not read it because he "would not soil [his] mind with such filth," but he knows "what the papers say about it." Even the title itself is more than he can bear, as he reads it to Octavius: "The Revolutionist's Handbook and Pocket Companion by John Tanner, M.I.R.C., Member of the Idle Rich Class." Then, for dramatic effect, *"he throws the book violently down on the table [. . .] relieved."*[20] Ramsden is being defined by his attitude toward Tanner's book and, by extension, by his attitude toward Tanner, whom he regards as a thoroughly corrupted and corrupting man. Tanner and his book bring out his limitations, but Ramsden justifies his position by declaring, "I draw the line at Anarchism and Free Love and that sort of thing."[21] When Octavius informs Ramsden that Ann has told Tanner that he will always be welcome in her house, Ramsden seeks help from the progressive, rational gods, starting off *"like a goaded ox in the direction of John Bright, in whose expression there is no sympathy for him. As he speaks he fumes down to Herbert Spencer, who receives him still more coldly."*[22] The implacability of Bright's and Spencer's statues symbolically parallels John Tanner's own imperviousness and rebuff of Ramsden.

After John Tanner enters and discovers that he is a coguardian with Ramsden of Ann, the literary motif continues to define the adversarial nature of their relation. Tanner goads Ramsden by referring to Ramsden's ideas as obsolete. "My ideas obsolete!!!!!!!" roars Ramsden. "Totally," confirms Tanner, who continues, "I had just finished an essay called Down with Government by the Greyhaired,"[23] the ideas of which he shared with Ann's father, who thereupon changed his will to include Tanner in Ann's guardianship.

After Tanner tells Octavius that Ramsden does not have "an idea in his head later than eighteen sixty," Ramsden sneers that he supposes Tanner's ideas are "set forth in that book."[24] Tanner, surprised to hear that Ramsden possesses a copy of his book, asks him what he thinks of it. "Do you suppose I would read such a book, sir?" replies Ramsden. Tanner is curious: "Then why did you buy it?" Ramsden replies, "I did not buy it, sir. It has been sent me by some foolish lady who seems to admire your views. I was about to dispose of it when Octavius interrupted me. I shall do so now, with your permission."[25] Shaw again uses a strong performative tableau to demonstrate the differences between the two, as Ramsden takes the book and *"throws it into the waste paper basket with such vehemence that Tanner recoils under the impression that it is being thrown at his head."*[26] Ramsden's action against Tanner's book is a violent rejection of Tanner and what he believes Tanner stands for; it could even be seen as a sublimation of the violence he would like to do to Tanner.

Tanner's book also becomes the battleground between Ramsden and Tanner over the issue of Ann. After Ramsden implies to Ann that Tanner has been guilty of "disgraceful action," Tanner explains to her that his book is the object of Ramsden's condemnation: "He considers that if your father had read my book, he wouldn't have appointed me. That book is the disgraceful action he has been talking about."[27] When Tanner then offers to withdraw from the guardianship, Ann announces, "I haven't read your book, Jack," whereupon Tanner, *"diving at the waste-paper basket and fishing*

the book out for her," requests her to "read it at once and decide."[28] But
Ramsden objects: "If I am to be your guardian, I positively forbid you to
read that book, Annie," and smites the table with his fist.[29] Ann then puts
the book on the table just smitten by Ramsden. Tanner creates the stale-
mate by offering, "suppose I order you to read it! What about your duty
to me?"[30] Ann diplomatically demurs that Jack would not deliberately put
her into a "painful dilemma" and brings about a momentary truce. While
the book has been the object of dramatic action and conflict, it actually
serves to provide the battleground for the differences between Ramsden
and Tanner.

As Ann interrogates the two guardians to see if they accept responsibility for her care, Ramsden objects to working with Tanner. When Ann
wants to know why, Tanner explains, "my views are too advanced for him,"
to which Ramsden retorts: "They are not."[31] When Ann asks Tanner if he
refuses to accept her as his ward, Tanner says he does not: "I suppose I
must face it," and, with the prompt of the face metaphor, turns away to face
"the bookcase, and stands there, moodily studying the titles of the volumes,"[32]
invoking the book and library motif again. Earlier, Ramsden had turned
to the statues of Bright and Spencer who coldly rebuffed him; Tanner the
literary man turns to books to escape the unpleasant task of working with
Ramsden.

It should also be noted as a part of the literary motif that Octavius wants
to be a poet, which provides Tanner an occasion to harangue Octavius in
a diatribe about the battle between the artist man and the mother woman.
"Of all human struggles there is none so treacherous and remorseless as
the struggle between the artist man and the mother woman."[33] Tanner's
own words will come back to haunt him as Ann begins her pursuit of him.

Shaw uses the library and the book motif in the first act of the play as a
way for the audience to gain an insight into Roebuck Ramsden and define
the difference between him and John Tanner. After act 1, Shaw uses the
garden to enhance the play's movement toward its main concern, the full
presentation of the Life Force. The final act of *Man and Superman* takes
place in a garden where the play's final meaning emerges, but before the
play arrives there, two other significant garden usages intervene. Act 2
takes place in the "park" of a country house in Richmond, and act 3 is set
among the mountains and olive trees of the Sierra Nevada.

The New Man and the Machine in the Garden

Act 2 opens with Shaw's stage directions, which point out that *"on the carriage drive in the park of a country house near Richmond an open touring car has broken down. It stands in front of a clump of trees round which the drive sweeps to the house,"*[34] a relatively pastoral setting on the grounds surrounding a country house. As the scene proceeds, we discover that John Tanner is talking to *"a pair of supine legs in dungaree overalls which protrude from beneath the machine."*[35] The legs, we soon find out, belong to the car's chauffeur, Henry Straker, who becomes a significant secondary character at this point in the play. Shaw seems to be working with several concepts in the second act. The image of the car, which Shaw refers to as *"the machine,"*[36] which Shaw carefully locates in the *"park of a country house"* with *"a clump of trees"* beside it, presents a very clear picture of a machine in a garden park, amid a nature setting. A number of ideas seem to converge on this tableau composed of Henry Straker (the New Man), a machine, and a garden, and these three items form the basis of several central motifs in the setting and vital points in the plot for the remainder of act 2 and on to the end of the play.

José Ortega y Gasset, in his *Revolt of the Masses,* uses the term *"Naturmensch"* to describe a new kind of man. "The new man wants his motor-car, and enjoys it, but he believes that it is the spontaneous fruit of an Edenic tree."[37] Ortega y Gasset describes precisely Shaw's scene here as well as the principal elements in the development of the remainder of the plot: the New Man, the motorcar, and the Edenic tree. Labeling Henry Straker as "the New Man"[38] and admitting that he is a slave to Henry because he is a "slave of that car," Tanner notes, "this chap has been educated . . . [and] he knows that we haven't."[39] While Shaw is taking a jab at the upper-class education of Eton, Oxford, and Cambridge, Tanner praises the New Man: "the arrogance of his pride in being an engineer, would appall you."[40] Henry clarifies that his education is from the Polytechnic, where they "teach you to be an engineer or such like."[41] Tanner admits his own helplessness in the face of such a man, declaring that Straker "positively likes the car to break down because it brings out my gentlemanly helplessness and his workmanlike skill and resource."[42] The New Man's economic pragmatism is part of his character: "You'll get more out of me and a machine than you will out of twenty laborers, and not so much to drink either."[43] Shaw seems to have a sense that the future belongs to technology, and Henry Straker, as a technician and product of the Polytechnic Institute, is the New Man of the technological future, and intellectuals, such as Tanner, find themselves increasingly at their mercy.[44]

Straker, in some ways, is more perceptive and intuitive than the other characters, especially John Tanner, on some issues. After Straker "saunters off" to give Tanner and Octavius some privacy to "talk about your ladies," Tanner reflects on the fact that cultured persons have been for years "setting up a cry of the New Woman" without noticing the "advent of the New Man. Straker's the New Man."[45] When Octavius says that he wants to talk about Ann, Tanner points out how that "Straker knew even that."[46] A little later in the same conversation, Tanner underscores Henry's importance: "Now here am I; and here is the chap Enry Straker, the New Man. I loathe traveling; but I rather like Enry. He cares for nothing but tearing along in a leather coat and goggles, with two inches of dust all over him, at sixty miles an hour and the risk of his life and mine"—a comment that has significance later in the plot development. "Well, if I don't give him a thousand mile run at least once a fortnight I shall lose him. [...] I am Enry's slave."[47]

Unbeknownst to anyone else, except Ann Whitefield, Straker, in foreshadowing later events, instinctively knows that Ann has already set her sights on Tanner. After Straker reenters the scene and Tanner mentions something about Ann Whitefield, *"Straker suddenly begins whistling his favorite air with remarkable deliberation."*[48] Tanner turns to observe his behavior, but since Straker is *"busy with his paper,"* nothing comes of it at the moment. When Straker sees Ann approaching, he *"strolls away"* with the air of a man who knows he is no longer wanted.[49] Later, when Tanner informs Straker that "Miss Whitefield is supposed to be coming with me," Straker coolly replies, "so I gather."[50] In a scene that could well be the crisis of the act, because of the dramatic emphasis Shaw gives it, Tanner implies that Ann and Octavius will be happy to be left together, *"Straker looks at his principal with cool skepticism; then turns to the car whistling his favorite air."* When Tanner loses his patience with Straker and asks what he means by his whistling, *"Straker calmly resumes the melody and finishes it. Tanner politely hears it out before he again addresses Straker, this time with elaborate seriousness."*[51] Shaw allows the scene to slow down, to draw it out for emphasis, and let it gradually unfold to the moment of revelation. Straker's reply, then, to Tanner's question is, "It's not a bit o use. Mr. Robinson may as well give it up first as last." "Why?" demands Tanner, and Straker answers, "Cause she's arter summun else." "Bosh," says Tanner, "who else?"

"You," says Straker. When Tanner shows that he is stunned by such news, Straker is surprised to learn that Tanner is unaware of Ann's feelings for him. When Straker convinces him that it is the truth and Tanner invokes the bee and the spider metaphor, Straker puts it in perfect perspective: "I dunno about the bee and the spider. But the marked down victim, that's what you are and no mistake; and a jolly good job for you, too, I should say."[52]

Henry Straker, the New Man who "has been educated," has understood all along what Tanner was unaware of, brings the truth to Tanner's awareness, and provides a turning point in the plot. Needless to say, the resulting action unfolds exactly as Straker has foreseen it.

The *Naturmensch* is actually part of a much grander pattern that has evolved in Western civilization, as articulated in Leo Marx's *The Machine in the Garden: Technology and the Pastoral Ideal in America*. While Marx's focus is on the American experience, his study brings to attention a phenomenon going as far back as the end of the eighteenth century and the beginning of the industrial revolution in England, if not all the way back to Virgil's *Eclogues*. Not only is Henry Straker a depiction of the New Man, as identified by Ortega y Gasset, but also Shaw's use of mechanical technology in the park among the trees in this scene anticipates Marx's theory as well as that of many American writers. But other English writers anticipated even Shaw; as Marx points out, Wordsworth asked, "is then no nook of English ground secure / From rash assault?" in protesting the building of a railroad through the lake country, complaining that "we lay waste our power: / Little we see in nature that is ours."[53] Blake, too, asks,

> And did the Countenance Divine
> Shine forth upon our clouded hills?
> And was Jerusalem builded here
> Among these dark Satanic Mills?[54]

Marx begins his survey by placing Hawthorne in a reverie in the green woods of Sleepy Hollow, noting the verdant nature around him, when he writes, "but, hark! There is the whistle of the locomotive . . . no wonder that it gives such a startling shriek, since it brings the noisy world into the midst of our slumberous peace."[55] Emerson says, "I hear the whistle of the locomotive in the woods. Wherever that music comes it has its sequel. It is the voice of the civility of the Nineteenth Century saying, 'Here I am.'"[56] Marx observes that "so far from being unusual, in fact, the 'little event' doubtless belongs among the literary commonplaces of the age."[57] Marx is reminded of Thoreau in *Walden* as he sits in meditation when his woods are penetrated by the whistle of the locomotive, of Ishmael in *Moby Dick,* when he is exploring the interior of a beached whale when it transforms in his imagination into a New England textile mill, and of Huck and Jim, in Twain's masterpiece, floating down the Mississippi on their raft, when a monstrous steamboat suddenly bulges out of the night and smashes through their raft. Marx lists the American works that have dealt with a similar motif, such as *The Octopus, The Education of Henry Adams, The Great Gatsby, The Grapes of Wrath,* "The Bear," and of authors also—Whitman, Cather, Jewett, James, Anderson, O'Neill, Frost, Crane, Eliot, Dos Passos, Hemingway—indeed, adds Marx, "it is difficult to think of a major American writer upon whom the image of the machine's sudden appearance in the landscape has not exercised its fascination."[58] Marx observes that "the locomotive"—and one could easily put the automobile in the same category—"associated with fire, smoke, speed, iron, and noise, is the leading symbol of the new industrial power. It appears in the woods, suddenly shattering the harmony of the green hollow."[59]

Shaw was well attuned to his age and prophetically ahead of his times. His employment of the automobile here in a verdant park in *Man and Superman* places Shaw squarely in the middle of a Western tradition, as identified by Marx with the image of "the machine in the garden," that symbolizes one of the basic phenomena in Western civilization and communicates something of the nature and soul of the age, perhaps the single most dominant trend of modern Western culture.

Tanner's, and by extension Straker's, machine forms a prominent motif in the play. Like the locomotive train for some writers, the automobile's speed is emphasized and lauded. When Tanner informs Straker that Mr. Robinson is driving down "in his new American steam car," Straker is incensed that he had not been informed that they were "racin us dahn from London!" and wonders why Tanner had not told him so. Tanner admits, "because I've been told that this car is capable of 84 miles an hour; and I already know what you are capable of when there is a rival car on the road."[60] Even so, Tanner is astounded that they have "come from Hyde Park"— another garden—"Corner to Richmond in twenty-one minutes,"[61] but when he asks Octavius, after his arrival, if his steam car is a success, Octavius brags that they "came from Hyde Park Corner in seventeen minutes," whereupon Straker *"kicks the car with a groan of vexation."*[62] When Tanner tells Octavius that it took them "about three quarters of an hour or so," Straker remonstrates, "we could ha done it easy under fifteen."[63] While speed is a point of pride for the New Man, everyone is fascinated with the speed of the automobile.

The car, its speed, and the desire for motoring and traveling become important elements in the development of the plot. First, Straker insists that a car is supposed to be used often, while admiring Tanner's fast talking: "I wish I had a car that would go as fast as you can talk, Mr. Tanner." He adds, "What I say is that you lose money by a motor car unless you keep it working. Might as well ave a pram and a nussmaid to wheel you in it as that car and me if you don't git the last inch out of us both."[64]

Later, without realizing the consequences of what he is saying, Tanner tells Ann, "learn to enjoy a fast ride in a motor car instead of seeing nothing in it but an excuse for a detestable intrigue. Come with me to Marseilles and across to Algiers and to Biskra, at sixty miles an hour."[65] That will "make a woman out of you," says Jack as he finishes his sermon, to which Ann replies, "it would be delightful: thank you a thousand times, Jack. I'll come."[66] Jack is of course *"aghast,"* and he tries to back out of it: "if there's no harm in it there's no point in doing it."[67] The motor trip motif, here introduced, lays out the action for the balance of the play as the machine drives toward another spot in nature.

After Straker has convinced his employer that he, Tanner, is the "marked down victim" of Ann Whitefield, Tanner responds to Straker, "Henry Straker: the golden moment of your life has arrived."

STRAKER. What d'y'mean?

TANNER. That record to Biskra.

STRAKER. [*eagerly*] Yes?

TANNER. Break it.

STRAKER. [*rising to the height of his destiny*] D'y'mean it?

TANNER. I do.

STRAKER. When?

TANNER. Now. Is that machine ready to start? [...][B]reak the record from London to Dover or Folkestone; then across the channel and away like mad [...].

STRAKER. Garn! you're kiddin.

TANNER. [*resolutely*] Stay behind then. If you won't come I'll do it alone. [*He starts the motor*].[68]

The very simplicity and intensity of their interchange, with all the surging feelings below the surface, create the power of a dramatic turning point in the action, and the machine is the central instrument of the excitement. Its significance becomes even more striking with the realization that the machine is the instrument by which Jack Tanner is running away from the Life Force, another force of nature, and headed toward yet another garden where the Life Force will triumph.

The Garden in the Sierra Nevada

Act 3 begins with Shaw's description of an impressively beautiful scene in nature and a garden: *"Evening in the Sierra Nevada. Rolling slopes of brown with olive trees instead of apple trees in the cultivated patches, and occasional prickly pears instead of gorse and bracken in the wilds. Higher up, tall stone peaks and precipices, all handsome and distinguished. No wild nature here: rather a most aristocratic mountain landscape made by a fastidious artist-creator."*[69] The natural beauty of the scene is obviously important in Shaw's creative vision,[70] and into this lovely garden, Shaw again introduces the machine, which has spawned a new industry: brigands who rob travelers in automobiles. After Tanner is stopped and negotiates a ransom, he persuades Mendoza, leader of the brigands, that he is rich because "miserably poor people don't own motor cars."[71] Shaw prophetically introduces another aspect of the machine, the car as status symbol.[72]

In *Man and Superman*, Shaw shows that he is attuned to the age in which he lives and looks to the future by bringing an awareness of the increasing importance of technology, specifically the automobile, into people's lives. The automobile in this play becomes an integral part of the action, structure, and conflict as a vital part of the daily lives of the people. But beyond that, Shaw also places the automobile in the context of trees in the park, of the garden, and of nature itself, as an emblem of the transitional state of things in his world, which Marx would identify some half-century later in *The Machine in the Garden.*

The Garden of a Villa in Granada

The third element that Shaw introduces in act 3, in addition to the New Man and the machine, is the garden. Beyond the setting of nature and the gardens in the Sierra Nevada in Spain is the garden in act 4, the place to-ward which the automobiles have been carrying everyone.

The first words of Shaw's description of the set in act 4 read, *"the garden of a villa in Granada."*[73] Shaw, as is his usual habit, goes into meticulous detail in his precise description of the garden, a sure sign that this garden is of high importance to his purposes. After noting that *"this particular garden is on a hill opposite the Alhambra"*[74] and that the villa is *"expensive and pretentious,"* Shaw comes to the garden itself.

> *If we stand on the lawn at the foot of the garden and look uphill, our horizon is the stone balustrade of a flagged platform on the edge of infinite space at the top hill. Between us and this platform is a flower garden with a circular basin and fountain in the centre, surrounded by geometrical flower beds, gravel paths, and clipped yew trees in the genteelest order. The garden is higher than our lawn; so we reach it by a few steps in the middle of the embankment. The platform is higher again than the garden, from which we mount a couple more steps to look over the balustrade at a fine view of the town up the valley and of the hills that stretch away beyond it to where, in the remotest distance, they become mountains.*[75]

After noting that the villa, from this direction, is located on the left, accessible by steps from the left-hand corner of the garden, Shaw then introduces the literary/book motif in the garden.

> *Returning from the platform through the garden and down again to the lawn [...] we find evidence of literary interests on the part of the tenants [...], on our left, a little iron garden table with books on it, mostly yellow-backed, and a chair beside it. A chair on the right has also a couple of open books on it.*[76]

Once again, Shaw has brought the library and the garden motifs together in one scene. Shaw also once again introduces the enclosed-garden idea by noting, when Straker enters through a little gate, that there is *"a paling on our left."* And, as always, it is a *"delightfully fine afternoon."*[77]

Northrop Frye, in his book *Words with Power,* notes the existence of certain features in the original, archetypal garden in Genesis: a "mist" or "fountain"; an "adam"; the garden with flowers and trees, "including the tree of life and the forbidden tree of knowledge"; four rivers; the animal world; woman made out of Adam's body; and a state of innocence from which they fall.[78] Frye also mentions, from Song of Songs, that the garden is "enclosed" ("a garden enclosed, a fountain sealed," *hortus conclusus, fons signatus*),[79] and the importance of ascending and descending *(secreta escala)*[80] as archetypal movement from the Bible and literature.[81]

Shaw's garden has many of the features of the archetypal original garden, including an adam (superman Tanner) and an eve (Life Force Ann).[82] It may also be seen as a foreshadowing of Shaw's critical use of the Garden of Eden in *Back to Methuselah*. In his description of this garden, Shaw specifies that the scene looks uphill to the horizon and that, figuring prominently, there are three levels in ascending order: the lawn below, the garden in the middle, and the balustrade at the top, with stairs leading up to each level, as well as stairs up into the villa itself. In the course of the scene, Shaw carefully traces the ascending and descending movements of the characters, as though on some type of ladder of love and beauty (the *secreta escala*).[83] Shaw also mentions, within the garden area, a *"flower garden,"* with a *"fountain in the centre,"* *"geometrical flower beds,"* and *"clipped yew trees."*[84] Frye suggests that the concept of the center and circumference is part of the final vision of the Apocalypse, with the "restored garden and the tree of life in the midst of it."[85] Shaw also includes a *"paling"* (Frye's "enclosed garden") with a little gate, which people use continuously during the scene. He also includes his literary motif, *"a little iron garden table with books on it,"* and several more *"open books"* on the adjoining chair— symbolic of the "tree of knowledge" in the garden.

In his stage directions throughout act 4, Shaw always places the primary action of any given scene on the lawn, below the garden and closest to the audience; all conversations take place on the lowest level of the stage. Meanwhile, characters not involved in the immediate action tend to ascend to the garden above to eavesdrop, to re-act, or to serve as backdrop to the conversation below, or they descend from the garden to become a part of the discussion. Amid all the changing of places and entrances and exits, there is much descending and ascending, a regular ladder of ascending and descending personnel, similar to the angels in Jacob's ladder (and the ladders of others). Whatever the ostensible topic of conversation in the garden or whomever it may involve, the real subject is relationships, specifically male and female relationships, union of man and woman, husband and wife, romantic love—and, by extrapolation, sex, the archetypal topic, according to Frye, of the garden.

In the course of act 4, being the resolution toward which everything in the play has been aiming, Shaw once again uses the idea of the machine in the garden as well as the garden as a place for discussing social position and acceptance. By the end, however, Shaw adds new symbolic meanings to the garden with the introduction of the Life Force. In one of his most explicit and elaborate discussions of the Life Force, Shaw significantly chooses a garden, a symbol of the earth, of fecundity, of nature, of the universe—of life.

In the opening of the act, when Violet converses with Hector Malone Sr., she introduces the machine into the garden by explaining Straker's position as chauffeur to John Tanner: "the driver of our automobile. He can drive a motor car at seventy miles an hour, and mend it when it breaks down. We are dependent on our motor cars; and our motor cars are dependent on him; so of course we are dependent on him."[86] Later, when Mr. Malone reads the note to Violet that she had written to his son, the machine in the garden appears again: "I have shammed a headache and have the garden all to myself. Jump into Jack's motor: Straker will rattle you here in a jiffy. Quick, quick, quick."[87]

In *Mrs. Warren's Profession,* the garden was identified as a place of social interchange, of social rank, and of social acceptability.[88] The same idea emerges here in this garden in Granada, Spain, hundreds of miles from the English gardens of respectability. Additionally and coincidentally, in both *Mrs. Warren's Profession* and *Man and Superman* the garden talk involves a parent's ambition for his or her child's social status. In the conversation between the senior Malone and Violet, the debate establishes Mr. Malone's determination to have his son marry someone with social rank, preferably with a title, while Violet defends herself as someone who holds "a social position as good as Hector's," even if it is without a title. Unbeknownst, of course, to Mr. Malone, Hector and Violet are already secretly married, which makes the tensions—and ironies—stronger. Mr. Malone informs her that Hector's social position is "just what I choose to buy for him" and that Hector may pick out the most historic house, castle, or abbey, and he, Mr. Malone, will buy it for him, provided Hector "wants it for a wife worthy of its traditions."[89] When Violet objects that any "well bred woman" can keep such a house for him, Mr. Malone points out, "no: she must be born into it."[90] He then explains that Hector's grandmother was a barefooted Irish girl who nursed Mr. Malone by a turf fire. "Let him marry another such, and I will not stint her marriage portion," says Mr. Malone, but, "let him raise himself socially with my money or raise somebody else: so long as there is a social profit somewhere, I'll regard my expenditure as justified. But there must be a profit for someone. A marriage with you would leave things just where they are."[91] Mr. Malone continues to explain his social ambition for Hector: "Me and me like are coming back to buy England; and we'll buy the best of it. I want no middle class properties and no middle class women for Hector."[92] Soon Hector himself joins the debate, defends his "position in English society," and is informed by his father, "your position has been got by my money."[93] Shaw humorously punctuates the garden/social-status talk when Mr. Malone, not knowing that Violet and Hector are married and thinking that Hector has been "makin love to a married woman," as he puts it, scolds Hector with, "you've picked up that habit of the British aristocracy, have you?"[94]

After the play passes beyond the resolution of the conflict between Mr. Malone, Hector, and Violet, it enters a new and final moment. Toward the end of the play, having usurped the garden from the Malones and everyone else, Tanner and Ann are left alone to bring the drama to its climax, the moment toward which the whole play has been moving, brought there by means of the automobile, the machine. Shaw also moves the garden setting beyond the talk of social status and introduces, as noted above, a new theme in the garden, the Life Force and sex, and, in Shaw's variegated art, a new usage of the garden.

In Frye's archetypal interpretation of things, the garden is associated with love, the union of male and female, fecundity, reproduction, and sex. In deciphering the significance of the original garden in Genesis, Frye starts with the notion that Adam was first alone in the garden, and that the garden in this state is his female, the "Mother Earth" his partner. Eve, then, "is the incarnation of the garden itself in human form,"[95] "a metaphor in which Eve is to Adam what the garden of Eden was to the Adam preceding Eve,"[96] establishing "a metaphorical identity between the bride's body and the garden."[97] Sexual union suggests fertility, says Frye, and "the bride's body is thus associated with vineyards, gardens, flowers, and the awakening of nature in spring."[98] Also, the garden was a real paradisiacal existence before "God spoiled it all by creating Eve, a malicious act that made the expulsion from paradise inevitable,"[99] which is exactly how Tanner comes to view what happens in this garden. Moreover, the sky is associated with the male and the earth with the female.[100] Frye draws upon numerous usages of these patterns, not only from the Bible, classical mythology, and classical writers such as Plato, Virgil, Ovid, and Dante but also from many English poets as well, such as the author of *The Pearl*, Campion, Marvell,

Milton, Blake, Shelley, Tennyson, Morris, and Lewis Carroll, to name only a few.

Shaw may not have been consciously aware of such connections, but he was steeped in the literature, religious and nonreligious, of Western culture and was unconsciously influenced by his vast reading. Shaw was a genius who trusted his unconscious and insisted that his plays were written by his higher self, what he of course termed the Life Force (Jung, Frye, and others would call it the racial memory wherein resides archetypes). Moreover, Shaw himself gives some license to a mythic or archetypal reading when he says, in describing Octavius's feelings about Ann, that *"the puny limits of individual consciousness are suddenly made infinite by a mystic memory of the whole life of the race to its beginnings in the east."*[101] Many of the patterns that Frye delineates seem to come forth in Shaw's garden in *Man and Superman,* and his use of the garden here takes a different and new turn.

Appropriately, then, Tanner's and Ann's conversation in the garden, ostensibly about the Life Force, is, beneath the surface talk, a dialogue about sex. After Tanner has shouted to Ann that he absolutely "WON'T marry you," and Ann calmly tells him that he does not have to get married if he does not want to, Tanner begins ever so slightly to acquiesce: "We do the world's will, not our own. I have a frightful feeling that I shall let myself be married because it is the world's will that you should have a husband."[102] After Tanner has explained to Ann that marriage to him is apostasy but admits grudgingly that Ann is attractive, she responds with, "Why are you trying to fascinate me, Jack, if you don't want to marry me?" Tanner explains, "The Life Force. I am in the grip of the Life Force."[103]

When Ann explains that it was she who chose Tanner to be her guardian, Tanner perceives the truth: "The trap was laid from the beginning." Ann demurs, "from the beginning—from our childhood—for both of us—by the Life Force."[104] Jack finally capitulates to Ann, to the Life Force, and to the garden as a symbol of sex and love: "I love you. The Life Force enchants me: I have the *whole world* [emphasis added] in my arms when I clasp you [suggesting the woman as Mother Earth]. But I am fighting for my freedom, for my honor, for myself, one and indivisible." The wise Ann placates him, saying, "your happiness will be worth them all."[105]

With all this talk of elemental matters, of love and mating, and of being in the grip of the Life Force, Shaw adds another dimension to the use of the garden in *Man and Superman,* for it could well be seen that Tanner and Ann, as original superman and superwoman,[106] are acting out the original

Adam and Eve situation. Ann, as Eve, is tempting Tanner, as Adam, with sexuality, and such temptation, according to Frye, leads to their expulsion from Eden. It is Eve, according to Northrop Frye, who makes "the expulsion from paradise inevitable."[107] The fall is from a state of innocence into a state of knowledge, from blissful happiness (in the sense of "ignorance is bliss") into one of awareness of the pain of this world. Tanner, who insists that he is "not happy," clearly views it as a fall when he describes his new condition: "What we have both done this afternoon is to renounce happiness, renounce freedom, renounce tranquility, above all, renounce the romantic possibilities of an unknown future, for the cares of a household and a family."[108] Tanner sees it as an expulsion from his own little garden of happiness, and this tale stands, perhaps, as Shaw's version of the story in Genesis. The license for such a hypothesis comes from Shaw himself, who invokes the idea that Octavius's feelings for Ann go *"even back to the paradise from which it fell."*[109]

Shaw adds another dimension in associating the female (Ann) with the earth: In a comic moment, Ann, when she announces to everyone, "I have promised to marry Jack," swoons and falls to the ground. Much consternation ensues, as several attempts are made by various other characters to revive her, until finally Ann asks Violet if Jack said anything when she fainted, to which Violet replies, "no." Ann then gives a sigh of relief and lies back down on the earth. When Mrs. Whitefield thinks that she has fainted again, Ann, lying in her *"supine"* position by choice, says only, "I'm quite happy."[110] She is content to continue lying on the ground, her connection with Mother Earth established, until Jack commands her to get up.

In *Man and Superman,* Shaw begins his play in a library and ends it in a garden. In the first act, Shaw takes great pains to delineate the person of Roebuck Ramsden, who dominates much of the action in his own library. In the remainder of the play, John Tanner, even though he made his presence known in the first act, emerges as the main character of the action and a demonstration of the play's themes, while Ramsden, although still present onstage at the end, retreats into the background with hardly a word to say, not even words to antagonize or criticize Tanner. Meanwhile, Shaw has used both the library and the garden to further refine his vision of the superman and the Life Force, has endowed these settings with deeper significances beyond their mere presence, and supplements his former usages of these two settings.

6

Major Barbara

The Salvation Army's "Garden" and Cusins's Books

In his second and third decades of writing, comprising his works from *Major Barbara* to *Back to Methuselah,* from around 1906 to about 1922 and covering a little over the first two decades of the twentieth century, Shaw continued to explore new usages of gardens and libraries. The major plays treated by this study out of this period are *Major Barbara, Misalliance, Heartbreak House,* and *Back to Methuselah.* Some of the other well-known plays from this period include *The Doctor's Dilemma* and *Pygmalion,* while *Saint Joan* and *Too True to Be Good* come a little later, but gardens and libraries are used most prominently in the four plays chosen. What is particularly relevant, and more to the point, is that Shaw, in his middle years and his more mature works, continues to find new ways in which to use gardens and libraries.

   Major Barbara has always presented audiences and critics with a challenge. As Eric Bentley, the sage of the modern drama, says, "*Major Barbara* is a play we all stumble over."[1] Alfred Turco adds that "this drama poses enormous critical difficulties,"[2] and Robert Jordan calls Undershaft a "strange figure."[3] Critics also disagree over what the play concerns itself with. Some—to cite only a few from among many differing opinions— have said that the play deals with "the problem of maturity,"[4] that the play speaks "not so much about money as about power,"[5] that it deals with the "corrupting effects of power,"[6] or that it presents a study of the "nutritional urge" as represented in Undershaft.[7] Shaw, apparently, would be puzzled by these kinds of comments, for he wrote in his preface to the play that Undershaft should not "perplex you in the least," that he becomes "quite intelligible," and that what he, Shaw, does in the play is really quite simple.[8]

The difficulty for critics seems to arise from the fact that they do not take Shaw at his word, as typified, for example, by J. L. Wisenthal when he argues that Shaw's preface is "misleading."[9]

Shaw begins his essay with the general statement that security "cannot exist where the worst of dangers, the danger of poverty, hangs over everyone's head."[10] He then adds a more explicit statement, stating that what appears as new "is that article of Undershaft's religion which recognizes in Money the first need and in poverty the vilest sin of man and society."[11] In the play, Undershaft says that poverty is "the worst of crimes,"[12] and Shaw stresses it by noting that the concept forms a tenet of Undershaft's *religion*. If we accept that Shaw and Undershaft are not speaking metaphorically and hyperbolically but literally, we can begin to understand Shaw's position better. Shaw elaborates his point by stating that the "crying need of the nation" is "simply enough money" and the "evil to be attacked is . . . simply poverty."[13] Shaw then points out that once you "fix [your eyes] on this truth just under your nose," then "Andrew Undershaft's views will not perplex you in the least."[14]

In the play, Shaw merely works out his premise to its logical conclusion: If "poverty is the vilest sin of man," then it is viler than making weapons; thus, poverty persists as such an evil condition that building terrible weapons to make money is preferable to being poor. That demonstrates how destructive to human beings and the human spirit poverty is, so says Shaw—and his play.

Shaw says it another way in his preface: "Undershaft is simply a man who, having grasped the fact that poverty is a crime, knows that when society offered him the alternative to poverty of a lucrative trade in death and destruction, it offered him, not a choice between opulent villainy and humble virtue, but between energetic enterprise and cowardly infamy."[15]

Shaw further points out that all money "is bound up with crime, drink, prostitution, disease, and all the evil fruits of poverty,"[16] and manufacturing armaments, implies Shaw, becomes nothing more than another example of money's sulliedness. Thus, a double bind exists: Poverty is a crime, but all money is tainted; therefore, it really does not matter what course one takes to avoid being poor, as long one remains truthful about what one does.

Being cautious in interpreting Shaw's comments is not an unwise habit, for he himself warns that a writer may not always be conscious of what thesis his work may contain. Wisenthal advises that Shaw's explanations are "deliberately one-sided,"[17] and Bentley cautions that what Shaw's greatest fame rests on is producing "contradictions."[18] If, however, Shaw makes a declaration about one of his works, such as in his preface to *Major Barbara,* and then uses techniques such as setting to help develop his thesis, one may perhaps feel a little more confident that the play in fact says what he says it does. Larry Herold observes that Shaw, in thinking about future productions when he would not be present to direct it, as he did for the premiere, "tried to make his intentions with *Major Barbara* so explicit that no one could misinterpret them."[19] This meticulousness extends to the care Shaw gives to his set directions. And settings, we remember, are fundamental in communicating to an audience, in performance, the essence of the world the play presents as well as several subtle implications.

In *Major Barbara,* the garden motif appears in the form of two outdoor settings (the yard of the Salvation Army shelter and Perivale St. Andrews) and the library motif in the character of Cusins, the man of books and libraries, and Shaw employs these two motifs for the purpose of developing the statement of the play that poverty remains the "vilest sin of man and society" and that money is "the first need."[20]

Aside from house servants and an occasional working-class member, such as Alfred Doolittle in *Pygmalion,* Shaw rarely presents poverty on stage but chooses rather to show those who are the exploiters and beneficiaries of the capitalist system. As Louis Crompton points out, Shaw does not, like Zola or Gorki, "directly depict Nana plying her trade or slum-dwellers in the full degradation of their misery, but instead shows how the middle class, while purporting to hold such things in horror, in fact condones and even profits from them."[21] In Shaw's world, we see the gardens and libraries of those privileged people who are beneficiaries of the corruption in their society: slum landlords, brothel owners, military officers, gentry folk, ministers, heirs and heiresses, arms manufacturers, doctors, titled classes, underwear manufacturers, retired sea captains, and so on. Shaw usually depicts a world that is characterized by comfort, elegance, and affluence—a world of pleasant decor, lovely gardens, impeccable libraries, and sunny days. In *Major Barbara* he deviates from this practice, for here he is clearly developing the thesis about poverty that he articulated in his preface.

As we have previously established, the definition of *garden* can be stretched somewhat if the following characteristics are present: an outside setting, an enclosed space, tables and chairs (or benches) present, and people leisurely eating and engaging in conversation. We remember, too, that this setting is a garden for poor people only, for we see in the West Ham Salvation Army shelter—one of the few times in all the works of Shaw—the lives of the impoverished citizens, their miserable plight, their sorrowful stories, their insecurity, their distorted values and con games, their struggles, their resentment and anger, and, above all, the violence that poverty breeds. The world of the English garden as a sign of respectability and as a place of social intercourse has vanished, and in its place appears an outdoor scene, the Salvation Army "yard," which is the only outdoor facility available to the impoverished wherein they engage in gardenlike activities.

Shaw's description continues: It *"is a grindingly cold raw January day."*[22] The difference strikes one immediately, for previously, in play after play, Shaw had given us gardens on days that were *"a fine afternoon in August"* (*Widowers' Houses*), a *"summer afternoon in a cottage garden"* and *"the sun shining from a cloudless sky"* (*Mrs. Warren's Profession*), *"a fine spring morning: the garden looks fresh and pretty"* (*Arms and the Man*), *"a fine morning in October 1894"* (*Candida*), and a *"delightfully fine afternoon"* (*Man and Superman*), to name just a few from the first decade of his playwriting career. Shaw usually has a strong predilection for beautiful weather in his comedies, but not when he decides to present poverty at its most destitute and painful. Shaw gives a detailed description of the "yard": *"The building itself, an old warehouse, is newly white-washed. Its gabled end projects into the yard in the middle, with a door on the ground floor, and another in the loft above it without any balcony or ladder, but with a pulley rigged over it for hoisting sacks."*[23]

The yard also has a stone horse trough and a "penthouse" to shield a table from the weather. No pretenses exist in this outdoor space, as well as no flowers, no expensive furniture, and no colorful decor. It is a place of necessity, the only place where the poor can interact leisurely. A man and a woman are seated at the table eating, not tea and crumpets, but bread (one slice each, with margarine and syrup) and diluted milk. The man is a *"workman out of employment"* and the woman *"is a commonplace old bundle of poverty and hard-worn humanity"* who looks sixty but is probably forty-five.[24] Shaw notes too that were these two rich people, *"they would be gloved and muffed and well wrapped up in furs and overcoats"* and that the background of grimy warehouses and leaden sky would *"drive any idle rich person straight to the Mediterranean."*[25] Shaw's contrastive reference to the wealthy class serves as a poignant reminder that we are amid poverty, that there are no warm clothes and no escape to warmer climates for the people in these conditions, and that the wealthy class (whether they make arms or anything else) have it far better than these poor wretched souls. As Crompton says, these people are "not a particularly cheerful, amusing, or attractive group of slum-dwellers,"[26] and what is more, adds Crompton, Shaw insists that "poverty is unequivocally *de*moralizing: its fruits are . . . hypocrisy, cynicism, and shattered self-respect, and . . . conscience-less brutality."[27]

The action of the scene coheres with the dreadful appearance of the outdoor environment. The characters who depend on the Salvation Army are "companions in misfortune," such as Snobby Price, an out-of-work painter, grainer, and finisher; Rummy Mitchens, an old-looking woman whose secrets have to be whispered to one lady at a time during her testimony; Peter Shirley, "a jumped-up, jerked-off, orspittle-turned-out incurable of an ole workin man"[28] (as Snobby describes him); and Bill Walker, a miserable, bullying, woman-hitting thug. These people, as depicted through the action, live in a world of ignorance, hardship, hunger, brutality, and violence. The blistering cold and marginally equipped yard reflect the lives of the people who gather there, and we remember it later when we are at Undershaft's pristine arms manufacturing village.

Not only are these indigents in a state of abject poverty, but also the institution itself struggles. The flashpoint of the act occurs when Barbara points out, "the General says we must close this shelter if we cant get more money,"[29] and the crisis of the act happens when Mrs. Baines chooses to accept the money from Bodger's Whiskey's and Undershaft's armament's profits rather than close the shelter. Barbara, realizing the truth of what her father had said earlier that "all religious organizations exist by selling themselves to the rich,"[30] abandons the Salvation Army to go to her father's armament factory.[31] The "garden" setting of act 2 emphasizes Shaw's unmistakable intention of showing onstage the differences between poverty and wealth, and, by labeling the "yard" as a "garden," it becomes a prism to bring out Shaw's intended irony and the virulence of his attack on the system.

After the sojourn in the yard of the Salvation Army shelter, we then move in act 3 to the countryside of Perivale St. Andrews, the location of the Undershaft Armament Works. Shaw's version of the "garden," or outdoor scene, here, again, becomes transformed, complex, and laden with irony. The picturesque, quaint little village provides the location of the manufacturing of weapons of violence, death, and destruction. The town *"lies between two Middlesex hills, half climbing the northern one. It is an almost smokeless town of white walls, roofs of narrow green slates or red tiles, tall trees, domes, campaniles, and slender chimney shafts, beautifully situated and beautiful in itself.* The best view of it is obtained from the crest of a slope about half a mile to the east, where the high explosives are dealt with [emphasis added]."[32] Interestingly, while it was a blisteringly cold January day at the Salvation Army shelter, Shaw makes absolutely no reference to the weather here in idyllic St. Andrew, even though it occurs at the same time of year.[33] In fact, Shaw gives the impression that all seems very pleasant: The town is *"beautifully situated and beautiful in itself."*[34] Shaw's unequal treatment of the two outdoor settings bespeaks his intention of depicting poverty for what it is.

This beautiful, natural setting on the surface masks the terror that operates beneath it. And the town, too, as Cusins says, "Everything perfect! wonderful! real!" and it is all "horribly, frightfully, immorally, unanswerably perfect,"[35] with nursing homes, schools, libraries, ballroom, banqueting chamber, and everything perfectly organized. Just as hypocrisy exists in the typical upper-class garden, as in *Mrs. Warren's Profession,* so it exists here, too. Underneath the pleasant, picturesque countryside surrounding St. Andrew and the perfectly organized society within the community and workplace lies, literally, a powder keg waiting to blow the place to pieces at the slightest mistake, a careless spark, or a lighted match.

Shaw has purposely set up a contrast and comparison between the "gardens" of St. Andrew and the Salvation Army. To underscore the comparison, he has chosen an outdoor setting for each, as opposed to being inside the Salvation Army or one of the armament buildings. The differences between the two are easily recognizable: the Salvation Army yard has poverty, misery, dependency, insecurity, and want; St. Andrew, on the surface, has the exact opposite—affluence, pleasantness, independence, security, satiety, and comfort.

So while a stark contrast between the two places exists on the surface, below the surface Shaw draws parallels. In both, money constitutes a necessity, clear organization exists (lest we forget that the Salvation Army is an organization), both serve a higher cause, and, the most important point of all, both suffer from the potential for destructiveness and violence. The settings help us to understand his point: If one thinks that making armaments supports a destructive and violent business, consider the brutality and violence that poverty breeds, and since no difference between the two exists, one may as well choose to make armaments and avoid poverty.

Comprehending what Shaw does with the setting also helps us gain an insight into Undershaft, who is one of Shaw's most compelling characters. While Wisenthal hedges his assessment that Undershaft is "by no means an unattractive character,"[36] other critics have been less restrained. A. M. Gibbs states flatly that Undershaft is "a magnificently impressive character,"[37] T. J. Matheson, allowing that he is "the most intellectually impressive character in *Major Barbara*," goes further to say that "he is unquestionably the most powerful and dominant character in the play" and quotes St. John Ervine's label that he is "the wisest person in the play."[38] Turco makes the assertion, which many seem to agree with, that he serves as "the hero of the play,"[39] and Michiyo Ishii goes so far as to declare that he speaks as "something close to [Shaw's] *raisonneur.*"[40]

Because Undershaft is such an extremely "impressive" character, some have been tempted to talk about him in terms of being "in the grip of the Life Force,"[41] of being a "slave of a cosmic force,"[42] of having a power of "virtually supernatural proportions,"[43] and of his being in a "state beyond the self."[44] Of course, critics also recognize that Undershaft is an agent for the forces of destructiveness and death. But, one may ask, how can someone be in the grip of the Life Force, a near superman, and simultaneously serve as an instrument of destruction and death?

Once again, a study of the settings helps to lead to the conclusion that the incomprehensibly powerful magnetism of Undershaft finds its origins in two factors: 1) his determination not to be poor, and 2) the destructive nature of mankind.

Of Undershaft's determination not to be poor, Shaw, in the preface, writes,

> In the millionaire Undershaft I have represented a man who has become intellectually and spiritually as well as practically conscious of the irresistible natural truth which we all abhor and repudiate, to wit, that the greatest of our evils, and the worst of our crimes is poverty, and that our first duty to which every other consideration should be sacrificed is not to be poor.[45]

Wisenthal observes that Undershaft is a "rare type" who has "the enormous force of will to determine not to be poor."[46] We can take that one step further by noting that that is one of the forces, his own will, that Undershaft is in touch with and which gives him his self-possession, his confidence, and his overwhelming power in the face of all opposition and objection. Thus, Shaw's depiction of the poverty at the Salvation Army shelter dramatically clarifies Undershaft's determination that poverty must be avoided at all costs. Louis Crompton notes that Undershaft has taken as his own the "stern old Scots slogan 'Thou shalt starve ere I starve.'"[47] That is a powerful determination and motivator, hardening Undershaft's unshakable will.

As noted above, critics are aware that Undershaft also seems to be in the grip of a force outside of himself, even referring to him as a "religious figure,"[48] and Shaw himself labeled it "Undershaft's religion."[49] Indeed, when Cusins asks Undershaft "what drives" the armaments factory, Undershaft answers him, "a will of which I am a part."[50] Moreover, in his preface, Shaw says that Undershaft has a sense that he is only the instrument of a Will "which uses him for purposes wider than his own" and that to people who have "that consciousness," "Undershaft the mystic [is] quite intelligible."[51] And what is this wider Will of which he is a part? The answer, one may conjecture, may be found in the "Don Juan in Hell" scene in *Man and Superman,* in which the Devil says that "in the arts of death [man] out does Nature herself," that man's "heart is in his weapons," that "Man measures his strength by his destructiveness," that "mankind is at its best when it is seeking means to destroy itself,"[52] that man is the "most destructive of all the destroyers," and that "the power that governs the earth is not the power of Life but of Death."[53] Thus, man's drive toward destructiveness and death is an awesome human force, and Undershaft, as the maker of the means to serve that force, is part of that larger Will, the Will "of which I am a part." The beauty of the place is made possible because of the enormous wealth of the Undershaft enterprise; the wealth of the Undershaft enterprise is made possible because of humankind's desire for weapons; the weapons are desirable because of humankind's destructiveness; ergo, humankind's destructiveness drives Undershaft, and, ironically, underlies the beauty of the place. In other words, violence and destructiveness are transcendent forces in human nature, and Undershaft merely meets that need. Moreover, the contrast between the beautiful surface of St. Andrew and the potential destructiveness below the surface is Shaw's emblem of man and society, which on the surface appears so pleasant and civilized while underneath lie the destructive forces of human nature that Undershaft serves.

Shaw's only other setting in *Major Barbara* is a library, located in Lady Britomart's house in Wilton Crest. This library setting generates the book motif that works itself out in the character of Cusins, because Cusins, as a professor of Greek, spends time in a library, and through him the library motif develops that also helps to resolve unanswered questions about him.

The play opens *"in the library in Lady Britomart Undershaft's house"*; Shaw immediately introduces irony by noting that Lady Britomart appears *"quite enlightened and liberal as to the books in the library,"* and when Stephen enters he takes up *"a Liberal weekly called The Speaker."*[54] While Lady Britomart belongs to the family of the Earl of Stevenage, she puts herself forward as a Whig, so that she will seem enlightened, progressive, and advanced, none of which she is. She remains as thoroughly conventional as they come. Louis Crompton points out that "Lady Britomart is an avowed believer in free speech and a democratic franchise, but every speech that she utters shows her native aristocratic spirit and natural masterfulness at odds with these ideals,"[55] and Crompton makes reference to "her conventional morality and her belief in the divine right of the aristocracy to rule the country."[56] Everything serves for appearances, as in so many of Shaw's library scenes (for example, the libraries of Sartorius, Petkoff, Morell, Ramsden, and so on). But Shaw in this play goes far beyond the physical presence of the library to achieve his purpose.

With the library setting established, Shaw then brings into this hypocritical show of erudition Cusins, who is comfortable among books and libraries and brings with him the ambience of bookishness, erudition, scholarship, and, especially, education, another motif in the play. As a classical scholar at the university, Cusins moves among books and the bookish traditions, his very trade depending on his familiarity with and mastery of books and libraries.[57]

The Undershaft tradition obligates Andrew Undershaft to choose a foundling as the inheritor of the business, but Andrew, in his search for the properly credentialed candidate, articulates his frustration, saying,

> every blessed foundling nowadays is snapped up in his infancy by
> Barnardo homes, or School Board officers, or Boards of Guardians;
> and if he shews the least ability he is fastened on by the schoolmaster;

trained to win scholarships like a racehorse; crammed with second-hand ideas; drilled and disciplined in docility and what they call good taste; and lamed for life so that he is fit for nothing but teaching.[58]

When Undershaft objects to the fact that Cusins is "an educated man" because it "is against the tradition," Cusins, in a response that could be articulating Shaw's own view of being self-taught, explains to Undershaft that "once in ten thousand times it happens that the schoolboy is a born master of what they try to teach him. Greek has not destroyed my mind; it has nourished it. Besides, I did not learn it at an English public school."[59]

Shaw uses Cusins and books to help develop his exposé of a favorite target—hypocrisy. Shaw does not, of course, portray Cusins as some type of idealized lover of books, pointing out that he has an *"appalling temper"* and is an *"intolerant person."*[60] Lady Britomart gives her own assessment of Cusins: "After all, nobody can say a word against Greek; it stamps a man at once as an educated gentleman,"[61] and, as we know, for Lady Britomart, appearances, especially those that make one invulnerable to exposure, are of prime importance. Cusins also condemns himself in his own words when he advises Undershaft to "study Greek," because Greek scholars are privileged men, even though "few of them know Greek," and "none of them know anything else," and he boasts that "their position is unchallengeable."[62] After all, "Greek is to a man of position what the hallmark is to silver,"[63] and thus, he infers, that man presents a distinguished outward appearance—the correct credential. Cusins, it seems, practices hypocrisy just as much as everyone else in society, and that recognition, revealed through the book motif, gives us an insight later into what will really happen when he inherits the armament factory.

Not only does unanimity of opinion among scholars not exist about Cusins, contradictions pervade the literature on him. About him in general, some praise Cusins for assuming "a central role,"[64] as being the "spiritual complement of Barbara" and "embodying intellect and will";[65] others speak of him as "a poet, an artist, a thinker," a "realist and reformer," and as having a "sense of high purpose,"[66] and as "a man of mature intelligence and cultivated tastes," a spokesman for the values of Western democratic society,[67] while others, such as Matheson, accuse him of "opportunism," "greed," and for being "shallow and unsubstantial."[68]

Through his portrayal of Cusins as a man of books, Shaw raises important issues. Cusins, as the eligible heir to the Undershaft business, apparently intends to accept Undershaft's offer to change his name to Andrew Undershaft, become heir to Undershaft's fortunes, and someday take over the Undershaft munitions factory, and he justifies his decision by talking about giving power to the common people. The primary question that arises in connection with Cusins becomes, what will he do when he inherits the Undershaft armament industry? Will he accept the armorer's creed of selling arms without regard to political positions or beliefs to whoever has the money to pay, or will he enter the business with the intent of changing the Undershaft industry, an intent he uses to justify accepting the offer?

Scholars do not agree on this question. On the one hand, some view Cusins and Barbara as "allies against Undershaft,"[69] as a couple who will oppose Undershaft's principles of money and gunpowder with their own principles of "poverty and nonviolence,"[70] and as a pair who are not really "converted to Undershaft's gospel of money and gunpowder" and as retaining "their own goals."[71] On the other hand, others see Cusins and Barbara as really having no principles of their own and succumbing to the allure of money and gunpowder. Matheson points out that Cusins, cynically, will "affiliate with any institution" as long as "it will aid him in the attainment of a prearranged end," which, says Matheson, is, for both Cusins and Barbara, power.[72] While Jordan admits that Cusins has the "decent liberal sentiments of hatred of war, [and] love of the common people," "these convictions are presented with no great force"[73] and do "not seem particularly forceful."[74] And then some see a compromise among the three taking place. Gibbs predicts an "alliance of the three as one of spiritually autonomous power,"[75] while Ishii views Cusins and Barbara as developing "into a larger, stronger, self with the aid of Undershaft,"[76] and Wisenthal believes that Cusins "will put the power of thought to practical use and his power . . . will increase rather than diminish when it combines with that of the Philistine world."[77]

The truth of the matter is that Cusins cannot have it both ways. He must either accept the principles of the armorer that have made the factory successful, powerful, and wealthy, or he will try to fulfill some lofty ideal through the factory, and the factory will fail. He cannot violate the creed that has made the business successful and still succeed. No one seems to have taken notice of what Jordan astutely points out: "The possibility that he [Cusins] might sell weapons only to those of whom he approves is firmly scotched by Undershaft."[78] When Lady Britomart suggests to

Cusins that he sell weapons to "people whose cause is right and just, and refuse them to foreigners and criminals,"[79] Undershaft says, *"determinedly,"* "No: none of that. You must keep the true faith of an Armorer, or you dont come in here," declaring, "from the moment when you become Andrew Undershaft, you will never do as you please again."[80] As Crompton says, "Cusins in the end chooses the 'reality and power' of the factory of death."[81]

Moreover, what some view as the silliest line in the whole play becomes Undershaft's tempting question to Cusins, "dare you make war on war?"[82] If one follows the logic of this, one can see that Undershaft uses this idealistic notion as merely a face-saving device by which Cusins can accept his offer: Undershaft knows that if an armorer makes war on war and succeeds, he has eliminated war and will no longer be able to sell weapons, and if he no longer sells weapons, he will no longer make money and will suffer impoverishment. (And how *does* an armorer make war on war, except by ceasing the manufacture of weapons with which wars can be fought, which would result in the same outcome?) Undershaft knows that Cusins is a naive idealist and shrewdly baits him into accepting the offer and on which basis Cusins justifies his decision to Barbara by saying, "Dare I make war on war? I dare. I must. I will."[83] The statement appears synonymous with the same hypocrisy he displayed in his attitude toward books and Greek. Undershaft is no fool. Basically Cusins and Barbara accept Undershaft's offer with all kinds of idealism and rationalizations in order to have access to the fortune the place provides, but Undershaft knows that, in order to avoid poverty and its horrors, in time their ideals will succumb to the unimaginable riches the place has to offer. Simply put, if Cusins violates the armorer's creed, he will no longer be making the money that Undershaft has made and his power will never materialize. Further, it should also be noted that the stretch for Cusins may not be all that great; after all, he is a Greek scholar, and Greek literature, including *The Iliad* and other texts, deals with epics whose main subject is commonly war, battles, slaughter, warriors, fighting, and so on; Shaw sarcastically invokes this theme in the title of *Arms and the Man* as an attack on the idealization of war.

Just as the Salvation Army must prostitute itself to Undershaft's money in order to survive, so Cusins sells himself and the scholar's life for Undershaft's millions. Thus, while Cusins appears at first as the only true man of books and libraries in the play, by the end of the play he has turned his back on them in order to make weapons that kill, and Shaw once again exploits the library motif, with attendant ironies, to expose hypocrisy, egoism, and debased human values.

Major Barbara marks yet another major variation in Shaw's usage of the garden and library settings. Before this, these two settings provided the physical setting in a number of plays while also taking on significances beyond their mere presence and lending insight into the characters, themes, and ideas. With *Major Barbara*, the physical settings themselves are less literally a garden and library, although they do remain present to a degree, and more of a metaphorical support for the play's statement that poverty is the "vilest sin" and the "worse crime," as dramatized in the "yard" or "garden" scene, and that hypocrisy is endemic in society, even among persons of books. After *Major Barbara*, he continues to use the garden and library in a great variety of ways, demonstrating astounding resourcefulness, as, for example, in *Misalliance, Heartbreak House,* and *Back to Methuselah.*

7

Misalliance

Gardens and Books as the Means to New Dramatic Forms

In *Misalliance,* it would seem at first glance that Shaw has abandoned the use of both gardens and libraries, for the sole onstage setting is *"a big hall with tiled flooring"* and a *"glass pavilion* [which] *springs from a bridgelike arch in the wall of the house."*[1] But that would be a mistake, for gardens and books are both present, but in a way unlike anything Shaw has attempted before: The garden, with which much interaction occurs, is outside and seen through the enormous glass pavilion, and books and libraries form a major portion of the conversations, especially discussions involving the host, John Tarleton. Furthermore, gardens and books are united in their mutual function of enabling Shaw to move in a new direction in both the style of the play and in his use of settings.

Some critics have theorized that Shaw, by the time of the composition of *Misalliance,* is in fact exploring, for him, new theatrical territory and leaving his dramatic past behind. Stanley Kauffmann in particular, in an interview with Jane Crum, eloquently defends *Misalliance* as an example of Shaw involved in a new experimentation, pointing out that *Misalliance* "relies on an absurdity of circumstance that underscores the seriousness of what it's about" and is "the first major occurrence in Shaw of a subtext that runs to the end of his career—the idea of absurdity."[2] Kauffmann argues that up until roughly 1900, Shaw "took forms and modes that had prevailed in the English-speaking theater for a century," but that from 1900 on he was "much more interested in devising new dramatic shapes,"[3] the implication being that *Misalliance,* ten years after 1900, represents a centrifugal accumulation of Shaw's devising "new dramatic shapes." Kauffmann sees it as a "maturation" on Shaw's part as a result of "self-discovery."[4] Michael

Holroyd seems to validate Kauffmann's opinion when he states that Shaw "attempted to do something new" in *Misalliance* and quotes Shaw as saying that he made a conscious effort to attempt "a specially developed example of high comedy."[5] Holroyd also asserts that "the tone of the play changes from realism into magic realism,"[6] which, while being an anachronistic statement, does capture something of the nonrealistic nature of the play. And Rodelle Weintraub notes that the play has "fantastic incidents," that it has "a pervasive air of unreality, even of fantasy, hovering about it," and that it is like a "dream" in which "the subtext illuminates that story."[7] More specifically, on the subject of Shaw's use of setting in *Misalliance*, Kauffmann says that "there are settings in his later works . . . [that] are Beckettian in that they are realizations of mental attitudes,"[8] and Weintraub makes a fundamental observation when she asseverates that Shaw's "stage directions are often as important as the dialogue itself."[9] It is true that Shaw, in the plays of his first decade, is consciously in revolt against the contrivances of melodrama and "Sardoodledom," as he called it, and striving toward a degree of realism, yet there remains in all of Shaw's plays an element of unreality, to some degree or other, of something present beyond the surface reality. It is also true that *Misalliance* pushes this element a little further than he had yet done, and it provides him with an opportunity to use gardens and libraries in yet another innovative, creative way as he experiments with "absurdity" (Kauffmann), "magic realism" (Holroyd), or "unreality and fantasy" (Weintraub).

In describing the glass pavilion through which the garden is seen, Shaw begins by making us aware that the house is *"in Surrey, on the slope of Hindhead,"*[10] which we can view in the distance, a reminder that nature lies out there beyond the garden. The glass pavilion is *"a spacious half hemisphere of glass which forms a pavilion commanding the garden, and, beyond it, a barren but lovely landscape of hill profile with fir trees, commons of bracken and gorse, and wonderful cloud pictures"*[11]—more emphasis on nature. This view of the garden and nature beyond the pavilion remains present from start to finish, and the characters come and go through the pavilion into the garden for various reasons, thereby drawing the garden and nature into the play. Shaw describes it further: *"The glass pavilion springs from a bridge-like arch in the wall of the house, through which one comes into a big hall with tiled flooring."*[12] Shaw notes, too, that near a *"crate are open boxes of* garden games: *bowls and croquett"* (emphasis added).[13] After giving the details of the interior, with the exterior always present, Shaw tells us that *"nearly in the middle of the glass wall of the pavilion is a door giving on the garden.* [...] *At intervals round the pavilion are marble pillars with specimens of Viennese pottery on them, very flamboyant in colour and florid in design."*[14] Thus, visual emphasis is given to the garden by its being framed by the marble pillars and Viennese pottery as seen through the glass pavilion. This alignment of glass pavilion, garden, and nature serves the action with metaphorical significance, stressing the presence of nature's magic and motivating some of the characters. We also learn that while the owner of the home, John Tarleton, possesses great wealth, he prefers, according to his daughter Hypatia, to sit in his garden and meditate: "There's my father in the garden, meditating on his destiny."[15]

The glass pavilion, which frames the view of the garden and nature, lends the play an air of unreality and metaphorical suggestiveness in two ways: the surreal crash of the "aeroplane," with glass falling in the pavilion, and the sudden, glandularly driven magic of Hypatia's and Joey Percival's relationship, reminiscent of that of Ann Whitefield and John Tanner.

The incident of the airplane crashing into the glass greenhouse makes a startling dramatic presence, one of the most startling in modern drama, and it has aroused speculation as to its meaning. Moreover, it divides the play in half wherein, as noted by others, before this incident *Misalliance* is like any other disquisitory play by Shaw, and after which the play takes on an air of surrealism and unrealistic conduct, referred to by Holroyd as a change in tone into "magic realism"[16] and by Kauffmann as an incongruity of "the likelihood of the circumstances."[17]

While an airplane crashing into a building is not unheard of in a technological world, the circumstances surrounding the incident make it seem unreal and fraught with significance: The plane, after knocking some glass out of the pavilion, crashes into the vinery in the garden; the occupants of the plane, defying all realistic odds, walk into the room completely unscathed ("Quite right. Not a scratch. I assure you I'm all right");[18] and the occupants, especially Lina, then proceed to make themselves at home, make demands on the owner of the house ("she wants a Bible and six oranges" and a "music stand"),[19] work their way into the lives of the people in the house (Lina with the men and Percival with Hypatia), and end up belittling everyone—as Tarleton puts it later, "you just see a nice house; drop in; scoop up the man's daughter; and off with you again."[20] Moreover, Shaw enhances the scene's significance with strong dramatic values, coming as it does in the dead center of the play and amid a quiet conversation about parent-child relations between Tarleton and Lord Summerhays: "*A shadow falls on the pavilion; and some of the glass at the top is shattered and falls on the floor. Tarleton and Lord Summerhays rush out through the pavilion into the garden.* [. . .] *An appalling crash of breaking glass is heard. Everybody shrieks.*"[21] Mrs. Tarleton's only concern, that "they'll spoil all the grapes," seems not only unfeeling but absurd. The ensuing dialogue also seems fantastical. The aviator says, "I'm afraid Ive knocked your vinery into a cocked hat. (*Effusively*) You don't mind, do you," to which Tarleton says, "Not a bit. Come in and have some tea. Stay to dinner. Stay over the week-end,"[22] even though Mrs. Tarleton ludicrously complains, "People have no right to do such things."[23] Both Tarletons' responses seem laughingly preposterous. And then the aviator admits that he does not know his passenger, who turns out to be a woman. Shaw is not, in fact, straining credulity but moving his dramatic art in a new and more complexly meaningful direction.

The surreal nature of the whole incident has, of course, led scholars to speculate on its meaning, assuming that it cannot be read literally. Weintraub, for example, likens the play to a "Freudian wish-fulfillment dream" that contains a "hidden meaning which needs to be unscrambled to find its original meaning."[24] She adds that "in the play . . . we see the story as it unfolds, and consciously or otherwise we understand the subtext that illuminates that story and aids us in comprehending what that story means."[25] Another example comes from Holroyd, who observes that the "invaders represent salvation, coming from the future not the past, the air and not the earth."[26] He adds that Lina "brings someone and takes someone away, brings Joey who mates with Hypatia and takes away Bentley."[27]

Several factors may be considered in attempting to interpret the scene's significance. The emphasis here is on nature and its contribution to one of the motifs of the play. First, as noted before, Shaw endows the garden and nature with potential meaning by framing the scene. Also, much emphasis, by means of repetition, is given to the fact that they have come from out of the sky, from out there in the universe, from out of nature: "A woman drops bang down out of the sky into my greenhouse";[28] the two of them "dropped down from the sky";[29] and "out of the sky,"[30] Tarleton wonderingly repeats. On earth, nature is stressed again, as Lord Summerhays describes Lina's rescue of Percival, saying she "caught you and turned you off into the flower bed, and then lighted beside you like a bird";[31] and Tarleton, unaware of what lies ahead for his daughter, knows that she "always wanted some adventure to drop out of the sky," which, unbeknownst to them, is happening to her.[32] The two characters' entrance into the house party from the world up there, the world of nature, represent two different aspects of nature: the biological (Percival's sexual relation with Hypatia) and the spiritual, the Life Force (Lina as a possible superman figure).

Hypatia's and Percival's relationship takes place in nature and evolves into an overtly physical and sexual one—in an amazingly, unrealistically short amount of time—and it is an entrance from the garden that introduces the beginning of their courtship. First, Hypatia, *"calling in the garden,"* summons Percival as she looks for him, and Percival *"runs in through the pavilion"* in flight from her. As Hypatia tries to get him to respond to her wooing, she notes that he "dropped down from the sky" and tells him, "you must come to the top of the hill and chase me through the bracken. You may kiss me if you catch me."[33] As he tries to resist, she insists, "we must play on the hill and race through the heather," "because we want to," she adds, explaining the glandular attraction of nature when he asks, "why?"[34] Percival then runs back out into nature *"through the pavilion,"* and *"she dashes off in pursuit,"*[35] while Tarleton watches the *"flying figures with amazement"* and *"is left staring after them as they rush away through the garden. He goes to the pavilion and looks up; but the heavens are empty,"*[36] implying that the universe has something to do with the phenomenon he is witnessing.

Much of the rest of the relationship between Hypatia and Percival is spent running through nature, appearing from time to time in the garden and pavilion and reminding us that what is transpiring is a force of nature. At one point we hear Hypatia's voice outside, *"a stifled half laugh, half scream,"* and then she *"is seen darting across the garden with Percival in hot pursuit."*[37] When she runs inside, with Percival still in pursuit, she makes the excuse, "Mr Percival has been chasing me down the hill."[38] Gunner cynically queries, "who chased him up it?"[39] and the audience knows the answer. Later, in a climactic, explanatory scene of the young couple's romance, after Hypatia and Percival dash in again, Hypatia announces, "Mr Percival chased me through the heather and kissed me," and Percival admits that he enjoyed it, although he did not initiate it and actually began by running away.[40] When Tarleton asks whether Patsy "can run faster than you," Percival describes a magical force of biology that caused her to run "faster and faster" and him to run "slower and slower," explaining, "these woods of yours are full of magic."[41] He then describes how the fern owl woos "its mate by striking its wings together twice and whistling that single note";[42] the energy that drives the fern owl "is what happened in the woods when I was running away. So I turned; and the pursuer became the pursued."[43] One of the functions of the garden imagery is to underscore the fact that simple biology is the active element between Hypatia and Percival. Percival supplants Bentley as Hypatia's lover because Bentley is not in touch with his physical nature as much as Percival is. The conclusion of the romance of course takes an economic turn when Percival admits that he does not have enough money to marry Hypatia, and she, stressing the physicality of the attraction, asks her father to "buy the brute for me."[44] Percival admits, "Patsy fascinates me," noting, "I apparently fascinate Patsy"[45]—"fascinate" in this case being an euphemism for biological attraction.

One other connection to the garden-nature-magic motif occurs when Tarleton expresses his desire to pursue Lina and says, "I steeled this evergreen heart of mine when I thought she was a princess [. . .]. She is accessible. Good."[46] When Lord Summerhays reminds Tarleton that he has a family and a position, Tarleton says, "No matter," "Theres magic in the night / When the heart is young"[47]—the magic here is the nature that lies outside in the garden.

As in so many of Shaw's plays, when a garden constitutes an important component of the setting of a play, it often is counterbalanced by the presence of a library in the setting. In *Misalliance,* no library appears as such on stage, but libraries are embedded inferentially in the play by means of a major literary motif, which includes discussions of libraries, books, ideas, and reading, and Tarleton's obsession, an *idée fixe* and literally described as a madness, lends an air of absurdity, grotesqueness, and farce as part of the play's nonrealistic style. But the book or library motif is presented through the character of Tarleton, whose ideas must be discussed as part of that motif.

In his opening description, Shaw immediately establishes a tableau of *"Johnny, reclining, novel in hand,"*[48] a description that foreshadows the oppositional attitudes of Johnny and his father over books and the several discussions about books and reading they will have. Moreover, within a few pages of the opening of the play, a discussion of libraries ensues when Lord Summerhays asks Johnny if his father is at home, and Johnny informs him, "no: he's opening one of his free libraries," and "he promised another free library last week."[49] In this same speech, Johnny provides a major character note for his father when he says, "he's mad on reading."[50] Later, when Tarleton is surprised by a would-be assassin, Tarleton tells him, "judging from your conversational style, I should think you must spend at least a shilling a week on romantic literature," to which the intruder replies, "where would I get a shilling a week to spend on books [...]? I get books at the Free Library." Tarleton is outraged: "What!!" he shouts, and the man explains, "The Free Library. Theres no harm in that." Tarleton ludicrously replies: "Ingrate! I supply you with free books [... to] persuade yourself that it's a fine thing to shoot me. I'll never give another penny to a Free Library."[51] Tarleton also is given to making ridiculous and self-contradictory statements, especially about books.

The sheer bulk of the reading references is quite overwhelming. Tarleton hardly has a conversation in which he is not advising someone to "read" one author or book or another. In fact, his imperative command to "read so and so" recurs like a refrain throughout. As a matter of fact, the word *read* (or *reader*) occurs some forty-eight times in the play; the word *book* appears some twelve times, *author* occurs some seven times, and other related book references, to *libraries, pages, writing, literature, letters, word, novelettes, novels, poet,* and *romances* punctuate the play. The list of authors actually mentioned or cited, mostly by Tarleton, covers a wide variety of literary fields: Darwin, Weismann, the Bible (some fifteen times), Browning, Ibsen, Shakespeare (his favorite referent), Chesterton, Mill, Jefferson, Kipling, Shelley, Mrs. Browning, Lombroso, Dickens, Tennyson, Pepys, Walt Whitman, Dr. Watts, Marcus Aurelius, Song of Solomon, the Psalms, *The Master Builder,* and even an author he refers to as "Whatshisname," a postmodernistic self-reference to Shaw himself.[52]

As a Shavian character, Tarleton presents an enigma, and one can never be sure what Shaw is up to. On the one hand, Tarleton is a successful and wealthy capitalist, although he downplays its importance, while on the other hand he is a man, as he says, of ideas, a free thinker. But his obsession with books, authors, and ideas makes him seem more like a caricature, like some type of Shavian joke, a character marginally in reality.[53] And one cannot help but wonder if he is not in fact a mere instrument of Shaw's satirical intent and not a fully realized dramatic character at all. And why does Shaw bestow upon Tarleton many of his favorite Shavian ideas?

As the founder of Tarleton's Underwear, he began, as Johnny tells us, "in a little hole of a shop in Leeds no bigger than our pantry down the passage there."[54] In spite of having made literally millions, making money has little or no interest for him. As a matter of fact, he has all along kept wishing that he would fail so that he could pursue a literary career:

> The circumstances that condemned me to keep a shop are the biggest tragedy in modern life. I ought to have been a writer. I'm essentially a man of ideas. When I was a young man I sometimes used to pray that I might fail, so that I should be justified in giving up business and doing something: something first-class. But it was no good: I couldn't fail. [...] First it was £250 more than last year. Then it was £700. Then it was £2000. Then I saw it was no use: Prometheus was chained to his rock.[55]

The ease with which he did it seems ridiculous and a parody of capitalists who work so hard to succeed.[56] When his son brags about the success of Tarleton's Underwear, Tarleton tells him, "it's not the underwear. The underwear be hanged! Anybody can make underwear. Anybody can sell underwear."[57] Even though he has himself written *The Romance of Business, or The Story of Tarleton's Underwear*, the business holds no romance for him. He confesses, "I'm getting sick of that old shop. Thirty-five years Ive had it: same blessed old stairs to go up and down every day: same old lot: same old game: sorry I ever started it now. Ill chuck it and try something else: something that will give a scope to all my faculties."[58] Certainly, Shaw is satirizing the dull, uncreative, and soul-numbing life of a capitalist.

What then is important to Tarleton? "Tarleton's ideas," he says, "that's what's done it. Ive often thought of putting that up over the shop."[59] Tarleton focuses on ideas: He proclaims that reading "educates us" and "opens our minds,"[60] he defends his "free library" as the "beginning of education,"[61] and he declares, "I'm essentially a man of ideas"[62] and "I believe in ideas."[63] Shaw's depiction of Tarleton is puzzling, to say the least, but Shaw does nothing without a reason. Tarleton wants to be an intellectual and a man of advanced thinking. In fact, what is curious about Tarleton is that many of his ideas come pretty close to being "Shavian," recognizable ideas on old age and death, parent-child relations, antiromanticism, democracy, antimaterialism, and the Life Force. Tarleton even believes in the concept of the superman, as evidenced by his statement, "still, you know, the superman may come. The superman's an idea. I believe in ideas. Read Whatshisname,"[64] another self-reference by Shaw. Tarleton himself, however, could never be a superman because he has sold out to money, he has not followed his Life Force, and he is only frustrated by his situation. One can only conclude that his grotesqueness and absurdity as a character arise from the fact that he has given his life to capitalistic pursuits while all the time longing to live a life of the intellect; perhaps it is a satirical statement on those who compromise their principles and lives. As Kauffmann points out, Tarleton "is a man who has made a fortune but, in his own view, has wasted his life."[65] Perhaps another part of Shaw's satirical strategy is that it takes a capitalist to condemn capitalism, for condemnation of capitalism by the poor would only sound like envy or bitterness. Moreover, Tarleton is portrayed as a man who longs for something more but who is weighed down by economics and the emptiness of a life spent pursuing money. Poverty, the worst crime, is not the only thing that kills the soul—so does a life spent serving the cause of capitalism. On another level, Shaw may be using Tarleton to attack conventionality, but, being a wealthy capitalist, Tarleton at the same time gains credibility with his fellow capitalists and gives greater force to Shaw's ideas. Shaw is just being Shaw, and he is using books, once again, to do it.

One of Tarleton's favorite subjects is old age and dying, about which Shaw himself had much to say, and their views are similar. Tarleton, in fact, on that subject, seems like Shaw's spokesperson. Gibbs says that Shaw "seemed impervious to grief and tended to view death with a kind of Ovidian detachment."[66] Gibbs also points out that for Shaw "death was the occasion for a renewed assertion of life"[67] and cites Louis Dubedat's death scene in *The Doctor's Dilemma* as an expression of Shaw's attitude. Dubedat says, "I used to be awfully afraid of death; but now it's come I have no fear;" [. . .] theres an indescribable peace."[68] About his own death, Shaw, late in life, said, "I look forward to my death, which cannot now be far off, as a good riddance."[69]

Tarleton shares the same detached attitude toward death. The first time the subject of age comes up, Tarleton says, "venerable be blown! Read your Darwin, my boy. Read your Weismann,"[70] August Weismann, a German biologist to whom Shaw made numerous references, especially in his correspondence with Gilbert Murray.[71] In discussing the Bible, Tarleton says, "if you want to understand old age scientifically, read Darwin and Weismann."[72] When his daughter, Hypatia, tells her father that "death is a rather unpleasant subject," Tarleton responds, "not a bit. Not scientifically. Scientifically it's a delightful subject." After again citing Weismann, he explains that cells identical to the ones "Adam christened in the Garden of

Eden" are still swimming around in a ditch, and "if big things like us didn't die, we'd crowd one another off the face of the globe[. . . .] And so death was introduced by Natural Selection. You get it out of your head, my lad, that I'm going to die because I'm wearing out or decaying. Theres no such thing as decay to a vital man. I shall clear out; but I shant decay."[73]

In response to his having wrinkles and white hair, Tarleton calls it "the repulsive mask. That, my boy, is another invention of Natural Selection to disgust young women with me, and give the lads a turn"[74]—nothing else.

Shaw's views on romanticism and romantic novels are widely documented and dramatized in his plays. *Arms and the Man,* which is an open assault on such notions, provides a perfect example, for Shaw's unmistakable purpose in the whole play is to debunk insipid idealism and romanticism, and Shaw makes it clear that Raina's romantic notions are based on the type of literature she reads.[75]

Tarleton also seems to take up Shaw's cause against romantic novels. As mentioned before, Tarleton wrote *The Romance of Business, or The Story of Tarleton's Underwear,*[76] but since we know that Tarleton himself scorns the business he is in, we can only assume that a book on the romance of business is a sneer at both romanticism and business. In Tarleton's encounter with Gunner he asks, "you read a good deal, don't you?" And when the boy mentions his "mother's doom," Tarleton points out, "there, you see! Doom! That's not good sense; but it's literature. [. . .] When I was your age I read books of that sort by the bushel: the Doom sort,"[77] and then Tarleton accuses him of wanting "to be the hero of a romance and to get into the papers," but Gunner, who, unbeknownst to Tarleton, is of a like mind with Tarleton: "Oh, rot! Do you think I read novelettes?"[78] Ironically, Gunner is more like Tarleton than either one of them knows. Later, he says, "don't you think, because I'm a clerk, that I'm not one of the intellectuals. I'm a reading man, a thinking man,"[79] sounding very much like his natural father, Tarleton, and providing one clue to Gunner's lineage.

Shaw's use of Tarleton as an instrument of satire is seen in his attack on romantic books. Tarleton and his son, Johnny, are both avid readers, but of very different kinds. Tarleton reads books for their ideas while Johnny reads romantic novels. We learn what kind of novel Johnny reads from Bentley, who, entering in the opening scene, says, "Look here: chuck away your silly week-end novel,"[80] and when Tarleton says to his son, "you don't cultivate your mind. You dont read," Johnny defends himself by saying, "Yes I do. I bet you what you like that, page for page, I read more than you

[. . .]. Only, I don't read the same books. I like a book with a plot in it. [. . .] I pay [the author] to amuse me and to take me out of myself and make me forget."[81] Shaw, ever the realist, mocks this attitude of escapism. Shaw also links the commercial aspect of romantic books, as well as plays, in their discussion about Kipling. Johnny says, as part of a much larger discussion, "I want to forget; and I pay another man to make me forget. If I buy a book or go to the theatre, I want to forget the shop and forget myself from the moment I go in to the moment I come out. That's what I pay my money for."[82] We know which side Shaw is on when Johnny criticizes authors who try to propagandize the reader, for that is precisely the kind of writing Shaw believed in. Johnny also attacks the superior position of authors as he declares, "the time has come for sane, healthy, unpretending men like me to make a stand against this conspiracy of the writing and talking and artistic lot to put us in the back row" and condemns writers as the "failures and refuse of business."[83] He also brags that if literature "would pay me to turn my hand to it" that he would not be a failure. In fact, Lord Summerhays, to extend the satire, observes that "all the really prosperous authors [. . .] have been very like" Johnny.[84] Lord Summerhays later unintentionally belittles romantic literature with the question that everyone is asking, "the great question [. . .]. The question that occupies all the novel readers and all the playgoers. The question they never get tired of [. . .]. The question [is] which particular young man some young woman will mate with."[85]

On the question of parent-child relationships, which is one of the main subjects of *Misalliance*,[86] Shaw always viewed the relation as a contentious one, based in part, most likely, on his relation with his own parents. With a mother who was preoccupied with her career and eventually abandoned her family, and a father, according to Shaw, who was an alcoholic, the likelihood exists that considerable distance separated him from his family. Shaw himself said, "my parents took no moral responsibility for me. I was just something that had happened to them inevitably and had to be put up with and supported. They did not worry themselves uselessly about my character and my future."[87] He continued, "I cannot remember having ever heard a single sentence uttered by my mother in the nature of moral or religious instruction" and that his father "taught me to regard him as an unsuccessful man with many undesirable habits, as a warning and not a model."[88] His daringly unconventional attitude about parent-child relations may best be illustrated by the story of his visit in May 1898 to a tiny schoolhouse where he met with children and "expatiated on the generally fraudulent nature of rules devised by grown-ups for children, and instructed them—to their joy—that their first duty in life was to disobey their parents."[89] From his plays themselves, one of the best examples of distant parent-child relations, from among many, is dramatized in *Mrs. Warren's Profession*, in the relationship between Kitty Warren and her daughter Vivie, who has spent most of her life in boarding schools, on her own, without a parent, and growing into an independent person. At first, Kitty wants to take possession of her daughter's life—"your way of life will be what I please, so it will"[90]—and claim her "rights" as a mother: "Have I no rights over you as your mother?"[91] But Vivie asserts her independence in the face of her mother's possessiveness: "From this time I go my own way in my own business and among my own friends. And you will go yours. Goodbye."[92] Later, Mrs. Warren desperately tries to hold on by attempting to make Vivie feel guilty and says, "youve no right to turn on me now and refuse to do your duty as a daughter."[93] Vivie scoffs at the idea—"my duty as a daughter! I thought we should come to that presently"[94]—and frankly informs her mother that she does not want a mother and that is the end of it, closing with, "I am bidding you goodbye now."[95] The relationship between Kitty Warren and Vivie typifies Shaw's treatment of parent-child relations, an attitude repeated with Tarleton and Johnny.

When Tarleton and Lord Summerhays broach the subject of child rearing, Tarleton brags that his "idea of bringing up a young girl has been rather a success" because he never treated her like a child and that he let her go "where she likes" and "let her read what she likes," although he does admit to the "difficult question this, of bringing up children."[96] Predictably, literature, reading, and books become the supporting evidence for Tarleton in such a discussion. He admits that when the time came for the traditional father-son discussion about the facts of life, Tarleton "had to leave books in his way."[97] He confesses, "you can't get over the fearful shyness of it," meaning the relation between parent and child, and he quotes a literary source: "Read Dickens." Lord Summerhays is stunned: "Are you serious?" And Tarleton explains, "I don't mean his books. Read his letters to his family. Read any man's letters to his children[. . . .] Theyre about hotels, scenery, about the weather[. . . .] Not a word about himself. Forced. Shy. Duty letters. All fit to be published; that says everything."[98] He adds, "I tell you theres a wall ten feet thick and ten miles high between parent and child."[99] After Lord Summerhays confesses that he did not have "time to be a father" and that he and his children are quite distant, Tarleton's reaction is once again in literary terms: "That's an idea, certainly. I don't think anybody has ever written about that."[100] He predicts, "depend on it, in a thousand years itll be considered bad form to know who your father and mother are."[101]

Finally, coming to Shaw's principal point, Tarleton articulates Shaw's ideas about capitalism, business, and materialism. Shaw lets his general opinion of capitalism be known in numerous places, one succinct articulation being in *The Spectator* of October 17, 1925:

> Capitalism. An economic system based on the demonstration [...] that if land be made the private property of a class, and the savings (called capital) which arise from this class having more than enough to live on be also jealously secured to the savers as private property [...] the result will be that every worker in the country will be able to earn a living wage and no more, [a condition that will be accompanied by] "appalling misery and crime, waste and idleness which it must with equal certainly produce."[102]

Some plays, such as *Heartbreak House*, draw attention to the fact that there is "no real difference between burglars [...] and the socially sanctioned burglars of capitalism,"[103] and Shaw points out that the capitalist system "destroys belief in 'any effective power but that of self-interest backed by force.'"[104] Shaw was fond of quoting Proudhon's dictum "property is theft,"[105] and he often repeated his own adage that "Capitalism, as practiced in England, is Plutocracy."[106] Tarleton, too, has something to say about capitalism, most of it in the form of a eulogy for his wasted life, as quoted earlier about being sick of that old shop, and that the biggest tragedy in the modern world is a life spent making money.[107] He sums it all up with his harshest criticism about "all this damned materialism: what good is it to anybody."[108]

Not only is Tarleton, who is a successful capitalist, opposed to materialism, but also he often comes very close to expressing his belief in a transcendence and in the spiritual realm, in something we recognize in Shaw as the Life Force. In a conversation with Bentley, he declares that "providence likes to be tempted. That's the secret of the successful man. Read Browning. Natural theology on an island, eh? [...] Prospero didn't even tempt Providence: he was Providence. That's one of Tarleton's ideas; and don't you forget it."[109] When Bentley tells him that he is "full of beef today," Tarleton responds with, "Beef be blowed. Joy of Life. Read Ibsen."[110] When Summerhays cautions him that "reading is a dangerous amusement," Tarleton defends reading by saying, "it's the beginning of education,"[111] whereupon he announces that he is going to meditate. In his absence, Johnny, a member of conventional society, whispers to the others: "Hes not quite all there [...] hes different from me,"[112] a sure sign of Shaw's approbation of Tarleton. Later in the play, when he is trying to woo Lina, Tarleton describes himself as having "a superabundance of vitality,"[113] another sure sign of the Life Force. He also soon comes to learn that Lina is a very spiritual person who focuses on her soul. She tells him that the purpose of the Bible is to "quiet my soul,"[114] and when Summerhays asks Lina why she prays, she answers, "to remind myself that I have a soul."[115] This resonates with Tarleton's inner self, and, in perhaps his most important speech in the play, he gleefully responds: "True. Fine. Good. Beautiful. [...] Ive got a soul: dont tell me I haven't. Cut me up and you cant find it. Cut up a steam engine and you cant find the steam. But, by George, it makes the engine go. Say what you will, Summerhays, the divine spark is a fact."[116] When Lord Summerhays rhetorically responds, "have I denied it?" Tarleton tells him that "our whole civilization is a denial of it. Read Walt Whitman."[117] Toward the end of the play, a conversation not involving Tarleton applies directly to him. When Summerhays says to Gunner, "you read a great deal," Gunner answers with, "Ive read more than any man in this room [...]. That's what's going to smash up your Capitalism";[118] all of Tarleton's talk about reading, his obsession with books, is a direct application of Gunner's remarks that reading is what is going to smash up capitalism, and it comes from the mouth of a capitalist. As is typical of Shaw, he likes to turn things inside out and upside down. In this case, he uses a highly successful capitalist (Tarleton) to attack capitalism, and he uses books as the primary weapon in his attack: the successful capitalist has a passion for books, and books will eventually smash up capitalism.

In sum, while *Misalliance* has no garden and no library onstage, the garden and books play a vital role in the play's meaning and demonstrate Shaw's resourcefulness as an artist. The garden provides the setting for the dramatization of the Life Force as acted out in Hypatia and Percival, books provide the anticapitalist capitalist with his weapon, and *Misalliance* represents another stage in Shaw's experimentations and anticipates a future kind of theatre, a more nonrealistic type of theatre. Gardens and books in this play also are used by Shaw in a new way in helping him achieve a more "Beckettian" (as described by Kauffmann), almost absurdist style of theatre.

8

Heartbreak House

"A Long Garden Seat on the West"

Toward the end of *Heartbreak House*, Hector Hushabye asks the unfathomable question, "how is all this going to end?"[1] Unbeknownst even to himself, he had already anticipated the answer when, at the beginning of act 3, his wife, Hesione, asks him, in response to the "splendid drumming in the sky," "what can it have been Hector?" to which he replies, "Heaven's threatening growl of disgust at us useless futile creatures. [*Fiercely*] I tell you, one of two things must happen. Either out of that darkness some new creation will come to supplant us as we have supplanted the animals, or the heavens will fall in thunder and destroy us."[2]

Nature, invention, human vileness, and creative evolution all conjoin in the speech: It is uttered in the garden, toward which the whole play has been moving, with the backdrop of nature ("heavens"), the theme of invention ("some new creation"), the revelation of the vileness of human invention when cut off from nature ("us useless futile creatures"), and the suggestion of creative evolution ("will supplant us as we have supplanted the animals"). In brief, the passage summarizes one of the play's themes: the baseness of human invention when alienated from, and contrasted with, nature's creativeness, as symbolized by the garden and nature.

Shaw's first words in the opening stage directions in act 1 focus on nature, of which the garden is a part. *"The hilly country in the middle of the north edge of Sussex, looking very pleasant on a fine evening at the end of September."* He continues, *"the windows are ship built with heavy timbering and run right across the room as continuously as the stability of the wall allows."*[3] In other words, in performance, it would be seen that nature forms the visual backdrop of the play and is given emphasis by being framed, with little obstruction, by the windows. On through the play, whenever Shaw gives stage directions, of which there are many, involving interaction between characters and the windows, the reader must keep in mind that the audience and the characters are gazing at the garden and the nature scene beyond. But nature, along with the garden, is also endowed with metaphorical suggestiveness, as will be seen. Other critics have noted the symbolic richness of the play. A. M. Gibbs points out that at "the beginning of the play the setting may seem no more than a whimsical piece of interior domestic design . . . [but] by the end it has become a powerful symbol of national destiny."[4] Stanley Weintraub states that Shaw intended to "keep the action on the symbolic level"[5] and that Shaw "charged" the play with symbolism, while Louis Crompton says that the play is "unsurpassed" for "the subtlety of its art, its depth of poetic feeling, and the fascination of its symbolism."[6]

After describing the interior of the house, Shaw returns to the view through the windows. *"The garden to which the glass doors lead dips to the south before the landscape rises again to the hills."*[7] He mentions an observatory and then gives a detailed description of what will be the setting for act 3: *"Between the observatory and the house is a flagstaff on a little esplanade, with a hammock on the east side and a long garden seat on the west."*[8] This scene is held before the audience's eyes in act 1 and becomes the location for the onstage action for the climactic scene.

Shaw's stress on the garden and nature could not be more emphatic. In fact, nature is described and referred to often, sometimes uncharacteristically of Shaw, in passages of startling beauty. Shotover tells Mangan, "you are beneath the dome of heaven, in the house of God [. . .]. Go out on the seas; climb the mountains; wander through the valleys";[9] he also tells Mangan, "the wide earth, the high seas, the spacious skies are waiting for you outside"; and when Mangan is threatening to leave, Ellie tells him, "It is a heavenly night: you can sleep on the heath."[10]

Shotover, who has spent his life out in nature on the seas, seems most affected by his experiences; he says, "I was ten times happier on the bridge in the typhoon, or frozen into Arctic ice for months in darkness,"[11] and, in his most eloquent articulation of his feelings about nature, he poeticizes: "at sea nothing happens to the sea. Nothing happens to the sky. The sun comes up from the east and goes down to the west. The moon grows from a sickle to an arc lamp, and comes later and later until she is lost in the light as other things are lost in the darkness. After the typhoon, the flying fish glitter in the sunshine like birds. It's amazing how they get along, all things considered."[12] The passage attracts attention to itself and serves the purpose of highlighting nature. Richard Hornby asserts that "these lines are the play's allegorical core."[13] In other nature passages, Hesione states, "it's pleasanter out of doors,"[14] Ariadne says, "it's cooler now" in the garden,[15] Hesione adds, in the last act, that it is "a lovely night,"[16] and Ellie feels that "its beauty soaks into my nerves"[17]—all of this is in stark contrast to the falling bombs at the end.

Nature and the garden are drawn into the onstage action by means of numerous exits and entrances, a fact that several scholars have noticed. Alfred Turco calculates that the first act alone has "nearly sixty entrances and exits—Shotover alone has close to twenty," and "fragmentation inevitably occurs";[18] Roger Wilkenfeld observes that the house "is an establishment with many doors" and many "complex entrances and exits";[19] while Sally Peters notices that the characters "enter scenes abruptly and exit just as suddenly, the fragmented action mirroring the brokenness of their experience."[20] More specifically, and heretofore unmentioned, Shaw's stage descriptions contain forty-six dramatic events of one kind or another that involve the garden: entering and exiting by the *"twin glass doors,"* sitting or standing at the window looking out, seeing people outside in the garden through the window, calling from the garden, whistling from the garden (*"a powerful whistle is heard"* from the garden), doing chores in the garden (Mazzini says that Shotover "is making Mangan help him with something in the garden"),[21] escorting people to or from the garden, gathering in the garden to visit in the final scene, hearing, from the garden, the sound of bombs, and experiencing bombs falling close by the garden. And some people seem to be directly affected by the garden. Shotover speculates that Mazzini Dunn, *"seen crossing the garden,"* has had "a strange conversion," and Dunn *"enters through the port window door, new washed and brushed, [. . .] smiling benevolently."*[22] After Ellie hypnotizes Mangan, she turns out the light and *"goes into the garden,"*[23] and returns *"from the garden, looking anything but happy."*[24] Hector, in his frustration, curses women and *"goes out into the garden."*[25]

With creative nature as a backdrop, the second motif, human invention, comes into play. While Turco opines that there exists the "near impossibility of offering an integrated account of the entire result,"[26] the theme of invention seems to provide one type of unity. Turco coincidentally notes the presence of invention in the play, although not as an overriding motif, and distinguishes between "two types of inventive faculty," Shotover's and Hector's, which "are analogous to the two varieties of artistic creativity that Shaw characteristically discerned: the great art of genius illuminating the previously unknowable and the small art of cleverness hiding what we don't want to know."[27] But the all-embracing motif is not the "great art of genius illuminating the previously unknowable," which is actually missing from the play, but the invention that Turco labels as the "small art of cleverness."

Invention, appearing in a large variety of guises, is so pervasive that it constitutes virtually all the action and is unnecessary to discuss here in detail. As we know, Shotover is himself an inventor, and most of what he invents, upon closer study, is revealed to be fraudulent; the "seventh degree of concentration" that he seeks is a fabrication and nothing more than a product of alcoholic delusions ("rum"), as are his pretensions to be busy by running in and out when all the while he is going to get a glass of rum; he tries to convince people that he sold his soul to the devil when the story was actually an invention to intimidate his "degraded" crew; and he also uses the trick of misidentification of various people, including his own daughter, to which Ariadne says that it is "very hard to feel quite sure that he really forgets."[28] But Shotover is not the only one who invents; nearly all the characters engage in such inventions as poses, lies, games, pretenses, delusions, sentiments, cleverness, dreams, and even literature.

In his opening stage directions, after giving a full description of the garden and nature scene, Shaw points out that *"between* [the port] *door and the stern gallery are bookshelves,"*[29] a description that introduces another kind of human invention, literature. The opening tableau of the play introduces a literary motif, with Ellie sitting at the window with a copy of Shakespeare's *Othello* in her hand, and the action of the play begins when the book falls off her lap and startles Nurse Guinness.

The importance of literature in this play has been amply noted, illustrated, and elaborated upon by such critics as Anthony Gibbs, Fred Stockholder, and Alfred Turco and need not be repeated here.[30] Suffice it to say simply that literature is another form of human invention, and this large literary motif is part of the overall "invention" theme of the play.[31]

In the middle act of *Heartbreak House,* a striking change comes over the play and its characters, which begins with a change in the setting. For act 2, Shaw specifies that the lights are turned up and *"the curtains are drawn."*[32] While these are rather simple stage descriptions, the implications are profound. As seen earlier, the stage directions of the first act feature a rear wall composed almost entirely of windows through which are seen the garden and nature scene beyond. An audience, having grown accustomed to the expansive nature scene, would be struck by the fact that the nature scene is gone and that the scene is exclusively interior, shut off from the outside. Coincidentally, the view of nature is gone and human invention takes an ugly turn. In act 2, Ellie concludes, based on what she has been witnessing, that it is "a vile world,"[33] and Hector says, "there is no sense in us. We are useless, dangerous and ought to be abolished."[34] A baser side of human conduct has been exposed.

After all the politeness in act 1, a different side of the characters emerges in act 2, beginning with a "cat fight" between Ellie and Hesione. After Hesione has told Ellie's father that Ellie should not marry Mangan, El-lie, *"turning vigorously on Hesione,"* shouts at her: "What the devil do you mean by making mischief with my father about Mangan?"[35] Hesione, *"losing her temper,"* rebukes Ellie: "Dont you dare speak to me like that, you little minx. Remember that you are in my house." "Stuff!" retorts El-lie, "Why dont you mind your own business? What is it to you whether I choose to marry Mangan or not?" Hesione defends herself: "Do you sup-pose you can bully me, you miserable little matrimonial adventurer?"[36] This surprising exchange occurs between two people who are supposedly friends. And then Ellie reveals her value system when she generalizes that "every woman who hasnt any money is a matrimonial adventurer" and attacks Hesione for picking up "men as if they were daisies," calls her a "siren," and asserts that she was "born to lead men by the nose."[37] Hesione wonders "how much longer" she "can stand living in this cruel, damnable world,"[38] and when Hesione attempts to smooth things over, Ellie persists in her hardness: "Dont slop and gush and be sentimental [. . .]. I dont care a damn about your calling me [sweet] names" and then insists that she wants "something iron, something stony, I dont care how cruel it is."[39] Ellie admits that she "was quite a nice girl this morning" but she is "now neither a girl nor particularly nice."[40] Critics have admitted that Ellie dis-plays a "hardheaded cynicism"[41] and a "new toughness,"[42] and that she is "hard and clear-eyed,"[43] but the reality is that she is more vicious than these polite descriptions make her out to be.

Two themes emerge out of this unpleasant squabble between Ellie and Hesione: first, the theme of the ruthlessness of women in the battle of the sexes, and second, the theme of reification, which becomes a dominant motif in this part of the play. The former comes to a climax at the end of act 2, when Randall tells Ariadne that "there is no animal in the world so hateful as a woman," and he calls her "a maddening devil" and a "demon."[44] Hector asks, "Is there any slavery on earth viler than this slavery of men to women?" and refers to women as "demon daughters,"[45] which seems to be the males' perception of females. Hector provides an illustration to Randall by pointing out that Ariadne "makes you her servant; and when pay-day comes around, she bilks you," and then, in the last words of the act, he cries out, with his fists in the air, "Oh women! women! women! Fall. Fall and crush."[46]

The reification theme emerges when Hesione and Ellie speak of Ellie's relationship with Mangan in merchandizing terms. Hesione warns Ellie, "he will be your owner, remember. If he buys you, he will make the bargain pay him and not you."[47] Ellie, as though bargaining for some commodity in the marketplace, haggles back: "I have more to give Boss Mangan than he has to give me: it is I who am buying him, and at a pretty good price too."[48] Ellie then, according to Shaw's stage directions, goes to the drawing table and *"fac[es] the windows,"*[49] over which the curtains have been drawn, clearly cut off from nature as she reveals her debased value system.

The ugliness of Ellie's and Hesione's conversation worsens as Hesione calls Ellie "a wicked sordid little beast" and threatens Ellie that if she marries Mangan, "you will never see Hector again."[50] But Ellie can play the same game and informs Hesione, "I nailed Mangan by telling him that if he did not marry me he should never see you again" and hurls a final insult at Hesione: "I should have made a man of Marcus, not a household pet."[51] The situation threatens to get physical when Hesione says, "of all the impudent little fiends I ever met! [. . .] What would you say if I were to box your ears?" "I should pull your hair,"[52] replies Ellie, who seems prepared to do so. When Ariadne later scolds Ellie, "How dare you?" and Ellie recoils with "I am not accustomed to being asked how dare I," Ariadne flings another insult: "Of course not. Anyone can see how badly you have been brought up";[53] she later calls Ellie "the most conceited young woman I have met since I came back to England."[54] The human capacity for the invention of vileness reaches its most extreme degree in act 2.

Ellie's practice of reification is emphasized through the use of more merchandizing imagery, and her planned exploitation of Mangan for financial gain is seen in her depraved justification to Shotover. Ellie equates the healthiness of the soul with money. She says that people used to think that "the less money you have, the more soul you have," but she knows that "a soul is a very expensive thing to keep."[55] Ellie equates one's spiritual health with material objects. When Shotover asks Ellie how much her soul "eats," she answers, "Oh, a lot. It eats music and pictures and books and mountains and lakes and beautiful things to wear and nice people to be with" and explains, "you cant have them without lots of money," and "that is why our souls are so horribly starved";[56] she insists that money will not be "thrown away on me." She further justifies her plans by explaining, "it is just because I want to save my soul that I am marrying for money."[57] Shotover wisely warns her again: "If you sell yourself, you deal your soul a blow that all the books and pictures and concerts and scenery in the world wont heal."[58] Crompton states that in order for Ellie to "save herself," she must remain "unbought,"[59] but for the moment, Ellie persists in her mercenary ways.

Ellie's and Hesione's treatment of Mangan encapsulates both the reification theme and the "ruthlessness of women" theme. The women regard Mangan as only an object to be used for their own financial convenience. Ellie boldly tells Mangan that "a woman's business is marriage. Why shouldnt I make a domestic convenience of you?"[60] In act 2, Ellie hypnotizes Mangan, and the tableau of Mangan sitting helplessly in a chair under the spell cast by Ellie dehumanizes him as well as symbolizes women's ruthless control over men. Hesione tells Mazzini Dunn to look at "the brute" who sits there hypnotized and asks, "Are you going to fling your delicate, sweet helpless child into such a beast's claws?"[61] While Mangan sits there, Ellie and Hesione talk about him literally as a physical object, but Mangan somehow seems to comprehend what they are saying, who upon awaking, confronts them: "So I'm an object am I? A thing, am I? I'm a fool" and "a disgusting old skinflint to be made a convenience of by designing women."[62] He somehow hears their "lies," "injustice and plotting and backbiting and slandering of me" as though he is not human,[63] and labeling their treatment of him as a "dirty low mean thing";[64] he is visibly upset and observes, "in this house a man's mind might as well be a football"—another object. Hesione, continuing the reification, says that he is not what she would "call a man. Only a Boss."[65] Mangan perceives the "thingness" of the women's attitude; he wonders if they "never think of anything about a man except what they can get out of him" and accuses them: "You werent even thinking that about me. You were only thinking whether your gloves would last."[66] The dehumanization of Mangan causes him to "break down" and he *"is heard sobbing"* as he goes into the garden. The ruthlessness of the women, which the men had talked about, is here depicted in their reification of Mangan.

Toward the end of act 2, all the characters drift little by little into the garden, and with everyone having exited into the garden, act 3 opens naturally enough in the garden. This had been anticipated when, amid all the vile talk, Hesione invites Randall to the garden: "It's pleasanter out of doors,"[67] and when Ariadne says, "I shall go into the garden: it's cooler now."[68] Once they are in the garden, the mood changes drastically. There seems to be a peace and calm, a cessation of agitation and hurling of insults. The nastiness has subsided. Sally Peters notes that the scene is "deceptively pastoral" and that there results a "progressive slowing of tempo,"[69] while Daniel Leary conjectures that the garden setting "proffers the promise of a new beginning."[70]

Nothing in the action has occurred that would account for this striking change, except their return to nature. The opening stage directions suggest a very tranquil scene, and nature is the subject. Lady Utterword lies *"voluptuously"* in the hammock, Captain Shotover is asleep on a long garden seat with Ellie leaning affectionately against him, and behind them in the gloom Hesione and Mangan are *"strolling about."*[71] The electric light glows *"like a moon in its opal globe"* and *"it is a fine still night, moonless."*[72] The first words are spoken by Lady Utterword: "What a lovely night! It seems made for us."[73] Hector rebukes Ariadne, "The night takes no interest in us. What are we to the night?" But Ellie takes up the cause of nature and praises its positive effect: "Its beauty soaks into my nerves. In the night there is peace for the old and hope for the young."[74] Peters states that the references to "the stars and heavens" "culminate in the dark garden,"[75] and Stockholder asserts that Ellie "focuses on the contemplative use of night."[76] This soothing quality of nature and its tranquility will provide ironic contrast with the exploding bombs at the end.

In the garden in act 3, a concern with truth, honesty, and reality dominates. Crompton labels the scene a "moment of truth,"[77] Peters notes that the "morally naked expose their souls,"[78] Wilkenfeld asserts that "now they confront one another in the garden,"[79] and Hornby says that Ellie's "extreme hunger in the first act represents more than a mere physical need: she is starved for truth."[80] Hector is brutally honest when he describes the group as "useless futile creatures,"[81] that "there is no sense in us. We are useless, dangerous, and ought to be abolished,"[82] and that "we are all fools."[83] After Mangan insists, "I'm telling you the raw truth,"[84] he begins to strip off his clothes, saying, "Let's all strip stark naked," because "we've stripped ourselves morally naked: well, let us strip ourselves physically naked as well."[85] Mangan's action seems to be a metaphorical expression of what is occurring here in the garden. Ellie too comes face-to-face with reality, admitting that "there seems to be nothing real in the world except my father and Shakespear." She has come to the realization that "Marcus's tigers are false; Mr Mangan's millions are false; there is nothing really strong and true about Hesione [...] and Lady Utterword's [hair] is too pretty to be real. The one thing that was left to me was the Captain's seventh degree of concentration; and that turns out to be—" "Rum," concedes the captain.[86] Then Captain Shotover explicitly articulates the symbolism of the garden when he advises everyone to "think of this garden in which you are not a dog barking to keep the truth out."[87] In other words, the garden is a place of truth, and the humans are not like dogs, dehumanized creatures, vainly barking to keep the truth out, but noble, intelligent beings who can confront truth and reality. In their return to nature, they behave as such. The truthfulness in the garden contrasts with the issue of invention, which is not needed when truth is present.

The final scene of *Heartbreak House* involves the dropping of bombs from the zeppelins flying over. On the one hand, the sound and the power of the zeppelins is emphasized. Hesione notes early in the act that "there was a sort of splendid drumming in the sky," which Hector interprets as "heaven's threatening growl of disgust."[88] When the airships come closer, Hesione refers to "the sound in the sky" as "splendid." "It's like an orchestra," she says, "it's like Beethoven," and Ellie amiably agrees: "By thunder, Hesione: it is Beethoven"—their animosity apparently having dissolved in nature's purifying air.[89] Nurse Guinness, by contrast, calls those responsible, in the airships, "murdering blackguards."[90] This pairing of the epitome of human inventiveness, Beethoven, and the human inventiveness of the destructive bombs completes the theme of invention. Human beings contain within them simultaneously the capacity for both good and evil, and great creating nature, represented by Shaw with a garden, remains the better influence.

9

Back to Methuselah

The Original Garden and a Library Too

It may be appropriate to end a study of Shaw's use of the garden setting, along with libraries, with yet another variation on his use of gardens and libraries and a play that draws upon the original garden of Western civilization, the Garden of Eden, and comes back to the same garden at the end of the play. The garden occupies two emphatic positions in this five-play cycle, the beginning and the end; the importance of it is unmistakable. Even though Shaw went on to write such major works as *Saint Joan* and *Too True to Be Good* after this, *Back to Methuselah* may be seen as a concluding effort of his garden usage. Vital to Shaw's ultimate statement are the components of this garden: the earth, Adam, Eve, the serpent—and Lilith, who may hold the key to Shaw's intentions.

Shaw finished writing *Back to Methuselah* by the end of May 1920, after he had apparently been working on it for a year and a half,[1] which, by Shaw's standards, is a considerable amount of time for him to spend composing a play, only *Man and Superman* having taken longer. Like *Heartbreak House,* it seems in part to be a product of War World I. The Theatre Guild produced it in its entirety at the Garrick Theatre in New York beginning February 27, 1922, with each complete performance of the cycle spanning three nights and running for nine weeks at a loss of $20,000 to the Theatre Guild.[2] Of the production, Shaw said that the same Life Force that guided the writer also operated in the producer, Lawrence Langner, "who ventured to produce this ruinously expensive and apparently noncommercial behemoth."[3]

As Shaw had foreseen, *Back to Methuselah* was neither a popular or commercial success, being among the least successful of his plays, nor has it been a great critical triumph. As Margery Morgan points out, "none of his plays has been more generally and strongly disliked both as drama and as doctrine," condemning it for "untheatricality, verbal incontinence and monstrous proportions"[4] and calling it "only marginally a play."[5] Louis Crompton, declaring it "the least popular of Shaw's major works," complains of the "austerity of its final vision" and specifically of the "artistic failure of the second, third, and fourth plays."[6] Maurice Valency accuses it of being "a tract in epic form"[7] and laments that, as a piece of theatre, "it leaves much to be desired."[8] James Agate, reviewing it in the *Sunday Times,* wrote that it is "one of the faultiest productions which has ever issued from a great mind" because of its "intolerable tedium," categorizing it as a "mistake."[9] Some critics have implied that the play deserves close study and attention, and those critics who see value in it meet on the common ground of the seriousness of its intention and its profundity. Margery Morgan, for example, in spite of her condemnations, admits that it is a "formidable achievement that sometimes touches greatness,"[10] while Desmond MacCarthy viewed it as a "tremendous effort of the imagination" because of Shaw's "obviously deep insight" and his attempt "to express his sense of the meaning of life."[11] Julie Sparks relates to Shaw's desire to be the "artist-prophet" in the tradition of Sophocles, Michelangelo, Bunyan, Goethe, and Ibsen,[12] agrees that a certain air of "sanctity and gravitas"[13] adheres to it, and allows for the possibility of "a significant new direction for theatre."[14] Additionally, some, such as J. C. Squire, have praised it in part for its artistic achievement, stating that the "craftsmanship of the Eden scene" is "astonishing," that "every sentence is revelatory and moves the action forward,"[15] that in places it "surpass[es] his previous best," and that the first and last plays of the five are "as effective in the theatre as anything that Mr. Shaw has ever done."[16]

Knowing Shaw's own attitude toward *Back to Methuselah* is helpful in discerning the relative importance of the play in Shaw's canon and the seriousness with which we must approach it. Sometimes it is not always easy to ascertain how seriously or literally we should take certain statements made by Shaw regarding his own works. Of his feelings about *Back to Methuselah,* there can be no doubt, and it is illustrated by an event that occurred in 1944. When Oxford University Press asked Shaw to choose the one work of all his works for publication as the five hundredth volume of its series of World's Classics, Shaw chose *Back to Methuselah.*[17] Valency believes that Shaw considered it to be "his major work" and that it "was to sum up everything he had so far written."[18] As a matter of fact, in the post-script to the Oxford edition, Shaw wrote that this play was "his master-piece."[19] Shaw claims that he was nothing more than a "note taker" in the grip of the Life Force,[20] and that, according to Valency, it "had been dic-tated to him as the Koran had been dictated to Mohammed, and that one day it would be appointed to be read in churches."[21] Valency concludes that Shaw regarded it as the "supreme attempt of the vital spirit to achieve self-consciousness. As such it was holy, a work of scriptural importance which was destined to supplement the Bible."[22] Valency describes Shaw on the subject as being in "sober earnest" and that he viewed himself as the "wise, stern, and all-seeing father, heavy with the need to admonish and to guide. It was a posture he had so far assumed chiefly in his prefaces and treatises."[23] Indeed, Squire in 1921 declared that in this play cycle, Shaw provides mankind with "the Bible of a new religion."[24]

The importance to Shaw of *Back to Methuselah* is a given; the issue to be dealt with is his purpose therein. Undoubtedly a number of interpre-tations have been given, most of which have valid claims and are backed with strong evidence. It is a complex play, and it offers more than one state-ment about life and the nature of things. It is about creative evolution and the Life Force, about the preeminence of the will and its role in longevity, about matter versus spirit, about "the human race as it exists at present,"[25] about the origin of evil and Shaw's "vision of the City of God,"[26] and about much more. A study of Shaw's use of the garden and the library in this play cycle should provide us with some new insights into Shaw's purpose.

In the Garden

Shaw begins *Back to Methuselah* with a stage description that states: *"The Garden of Eden. Afternoon. An immense serpent is sleeping with her head bur-ied in a thick bed of Johnswort, and her body coiled in apparently endless rings through the branches of a tree, which is already well grown, for the days of creation have been longer than our reckoning."*[27] At first the audience does not see her, but Shaw's alertness to performance values is seen in the man-ner by which he reveals the serpent by slow degrees, for at first *"she is not visible to anyone unaware of her presence, as her colors of green and brown make a perfect camouflage."*[28] After a brief scene between Adam and Eve, the serpent is ready to reveal herself, which she does in a startling fash-ion: *"The body of the serpent becomes visible, glowing with wonderful new colors. She rears her head from the bed of Johnswort, and speaks into Eve's ear in a strange seductively musical whisper."*[29] While the serpent is talking to Eve, *"she spreads a magnificent amethystine hood,"*[30] another stage in her unfolding. This is no ordinary conception of a snake. Once the serpent has fully revealed herself, one would, in recalling Shaw's original description of her presence, become keenly aware in a performance of the visually overpowering presence of the serpent in the stage picture, an *"immense"* creature with *"endless rings"* entwined in the branches of a tree, *"glowing"* with "wonderful new colors" and a *"magnificent amethystine hood."* Obviously Shaw intends for the serpent to have an overwhelming impact on the consciousness of the audience, just as the snake of *Genesis* has had a lasting impact on Western consciousness. In the Bible, the serpent is, aside from God, the central character, the activator, the catalyst of the action, and the shaper of human destiny. Beyond that, Shaw here stresses the power of the influence of the serpent on Adam and Eve and on the action of the play, for it is the serpent who teaches the couple many things, including new words (*dead, born, birth, life, kill, love, jealousy, fear, hope,* and so on), the background history about the beginning, instructions on how to use the will to create things, the importance of Lilith in the creation of Adam and Eve, and the "secret" of how to "conceive," as seen in the last lines of act 1 when the serpent *"begins whispering to her[;] Eve's face lights up with intense interest, which increases until an expression of overwhelming repugnance takes its place"* and *"she buries her face in her hands."*[31] And procreation begins. In some ways, as Shaw seems to emphasize, the serpent, along with Lilith, is more important in the story than Adam and Eve are, for it all starts with the serpent, who is beguiling, crafty, and persuasive (the word in Genesis is "subtle").

In the opening description, the serpent's head is *"buried in a thick bed of* Johnswort."[32] That Shaw specifically mentions Saint-John's-wort must have some significance, given his propensity for endowing every detail with meaning. Indeed, the plant has a long history as a medicinal herb in Europe, and an even longer history as a plant that wards off evil spirits. Its role as a good luck charm and banisher of evil is illustrated in one of its many common names, "chase-devil," which is rather appropriate, since a "devil" does not seem to be present at all in Shaw's version. Medicinally, Saint-John's-wort is even today widely known as an herbal treatment for depression. The serpent is also appropriately associated with an antidepressant since she brings instructions to Adam and Eve on a fairly effective remedy for depression—sex.

Shaw is rather faithful to the story of Genesis in many ways, including Adam's struggle with briars and thistles, Eve as faithful helpmate, Cain as the first murderer, and Adam as a laborer of the earth. A cursory look at the book of Genesis shows that the earth and the ground are vitally important to the story. God created the earth, "dry land," on the third day; the earth produced grass, herbs, and fruit trees also on the third day; the earth brought "forth the living creature after his kind" on the sixth day; and there "went up a mist" from the earth to water "the whole face of the ground"; then God, after he rested, "formed man of the dust of the ground," "and out of the ground made the Lord God to grow every tree that is pleasant to the sight," "and out of the ground the Lord God formed every beast of the field, and every fowl of the air"; and after Adam and Eve eat of the forbidden fruit, God curses the serpent to eat dust "all the days of thy life," and to Adam he says, "cursed is the ground for thy sake; in sorrow shalt thou eat of it all the days of thy life," until he returns to the ground, "for dust thou art and unto dust shalt thou return." And then God exiles Adam and Eve from the garden to work the ground: "the Lord God sent him forth from the garden of Eden, to till the ground from whence he was taken." As a result of God's curse, the earth also produces thorns and thistles.

The dominance of the earth in Genesis was not lost on Shaw, for the ground provides the main activity for Adam, "digging," and the chief metaphor for the disagreement between Adam and Cain. In act 2 of *In the Beginning,* even though Adam and Eve have been cast out from the Garden of Eden, they are still in a garden, in this case a *"kitchen garden,"* and Adam dutifully obeys the biblical command to "till the ground," for Shaw's stage directions has Adam *"digging in the middle of the garden."*[33] After Cain arrives, who in *"pose, voice, and dress"* is *"insistently war-like,"* the ground provides the basis for the contention between Adam and his son. Cain scoffs at his father: "Still digging? Always dig, dig, dig. Sticking in the old furrow. [. . .] What should I be if I had stuck to the digging you taught me?" Adam, in reply, reminds Cain of his "brother's blood crying from the ground against you."[34] Cain smugly compares his present life to what his father taught him: "I dug and dug and dug. I cleared away the thistles and briars. I ate the fruits of the earth. I lived in the sweat of my brow, as you do. I was a fool."[35] From this point on, father and son engage in a debate, similar to the old medieval *debat,* pitting discussions of digging and farming against fighting and killing. The image of digging the ground occurs in some twenty conversations through the rest of the act, culminating with Adam stating, "I will dig, and live,"[36] while his wife berates Adam for being a fool with his incessant "digging."[37] Basically, the garden provides Shaw with both his fundamental subject and the basis for the philosophical difference between Adam and Cain.

Lilith

On the other hand, Shaw deviates in a major way from the Genesis story of the creation of Adam and Eve. The Bible clearly states that God "formed man of the dust of the ground and breathed into his nostrils the breath of life; and man became a living soul," and that later God put Adam into a "deep sleep" in order to take one of his ribs from which "made he a woman." In *Back to Methuselah,* Shaw never mentions God, not once, for God is totally absent. He does, however, introduce, by way of the serpent, the character of Lilith, who in his version of the story is responsible for creating Adam and Eve. The serpent tells Eve that Lilith "strove and strove and willed and willed [. . . and] lo! There was not one new Lilith but two: one like herself, the other like Adam. You were the one: Adam was the other."[38] Shaw, of course, does not invent things like this casually nor without a definite purpose. Thus Lilith, the present argument contends, holds the key to understanding one of Shaw's purposes in *Back to Methuselah,* especially considering that she is the last character on stage at the end of the whole cycle and delivering the final summation speech in a play that Shaw considered to be his "masterpiece." It seems that a critical question here is, what aspect of the Lilith legend does Shaw have in mind, using her so conclusively in his play?

Without going into an endlessly detailed study of the myth of Lilith, which has an ancient, complex, rich, and varied history, a consideration of the salient points may yield some clues. The myth is primarily of Jewish origin and has appeared in various texts, such as the Bible (one reference in Isaiah 34:14), the Midrash, the Talmud (with insertions by different rabbis through the centuries), the Kabbalah, Zohar, and even Medieval Christian writings. It has also appeared outside Jewish literature in Sumerian, Babylonian, Assyrian, Libyan, and other texts.

Several persistent beliefs appear in connection with Lilith's name. One says that she was Adam's first wife, created by God out of the same earth as Adam, but that a dispute developed between them because of her refusal to assume a supine position underneath Adam during intercourse, after which she blasphemed by uttering Yahweh's name and disappeared. By her refusal to be obedient to Adam, she introduced evil into the world. For many feminists, she represents the rebellion against the ancient patriarchal system. Other interpretations see her as Eve herself and some as the serpent. Various associations through the centuries cling to her name: She is associated with night, killing infants, harming pregnant women, and drinking blood. But the most powerful and persistent aspect of her myth is her association with men.

From the beginning, even in the case of Adam, she has been portrayed as very sexual, seductive, lustful, licentious, and tempting with her beauty and her long hair; she appears to men in their erotic dreams, she wanders about at night vexing the sons of men and causing them to defile themselves, she copulates with men in their sleep, causing them to have nocturnal emissions, and constantly seduces men.[39] She comes to represent the "powerfully sexual woman against whom men . . . ha[ve] few defenses";[40] she "demonstrates how, when unchecked, female sexuality is disruptive and destructive";[41] she, "much more than Eve, personifies the real (sexual) power women exercise over men";[42] and "she represents the deeper, darker fear men have of women and female sexuality."[43]

Over the years and into the modern age, this last portrayal of Lilith as exercising sexual power over men has come to dominate her identity, appearing as such in poems by Rossetti and Browning, which Shaw could well have known. Dante Gabriel Rossetti painted two different portraits of Lilith, one in 1863 and another in 1866, to which he attached the poem, "Lilith (for a Picture)," in which, after talking about her "enchanted hair" as the "first gold," the poet says that she "draws men to watch the bright net she can weave, / Till heart and body and life are in its hold"; the poem declares that her "spell [went] through him [the victim], and left his straight neck bent, / And round his heart one strangling golden hair."[44] Lilith is associated with ensnaring and entrapping men by means of her seductive power. Robert Browning, in his poem "Adam, Lilith and Eve," also portrays her as dangerous and deceptive: "I met your love with scorning," she brags, talks about the "venom" on her lips, and tempts him to strip "The mask from my soul with a kiss."[45] Over time, Lilith has morphed into a dangerous, controlling, ensnaring, seducing femme fatale. Surely this image has to be a part, somehow, of the association Shaw had in mind for his most crucial character.

Further, Shaw in any number of plays portrays female characters as quite strong, as instruments of the Life Force, or even potentially as a superman/woman. Vivie Warren, for example, although quite young, has the potential, through her fierce independence, to possibly become a superman/woman in the future; Candida Morell and Ann Whitefield are clearly in the service of the Life Force and appear stronger than the men around them (as Candida says of her husband and Marchbanks, "I give myself to the weaker of the two");[46] and Barbara Undershaft, while seeming to compromise herself by the end of the play, longs to serve a higher power. While the list goes on, still to come for Shaw, of course, is his greatest superman/woman creation of all, Saint Joan. Many of Shaw's women, as vessels of the Life Force, have a biological and, by extension, natural power.[47] But with Lilith, Shaw seems to be going a step further. Lilith, according to Shaw, is the creator of the first human beings, a godlike action. Is she an agent of God's? Is she God? Is she the representative of some abstract force, such as the Life Force, in the universe? Is Shaw basically saying that the ultimate force of the universe is feminine, a creating, controlling, and manipulating power, not just biologically but spiritually as well?

Eve and Lilith

The strength of woman becomes a major theme of act 2 of *In the Beginning*. Cain, in addition to his debate with his father over farming and killing, also debates with his mother over the relative strength of man and woman. On the subject of Eve's childbearing powers, Cain belittles his father, saying, "you make my father here your mere convenience, as you call it, for that. He has to dig for you, sweat for you, plod for you, like the ox who helps him to tear up the ground or the ass who carries his burdens for him. No woman shall make me live my father's life."[48]

When Cain boasts of how he has his wife under control, his mother states the real truth of the situation: "You her master! You are more her slave than Adam's ox or your own sheep-dog."[49] After pointing out that Cain risks his life while killing animals for his wife, Eve says, "You fight because you think that your fighting makes her admire and desire you. Fool:

she makes you fight because you bring her the ornaments and the treasures of those you have slain."[50]

When Cain brags that he has beaten his wife black and blue, his mother reminds him that it was because she looked at another man, and "then you groveled at her feet, and cried, and begged her to forgive you and were ten times more her slave than ever."[51] When Cain asserts that his wife loved him more than ever for it, his mother puts the face of truth on it: "You have no real strength in your bones nor sap in your flesh."[52] In spite of Cain's brashness, his mother makes it clear that he is deceiving himself and that his wife is in charge, the stronger of the two. The spirit of Lilith, speaking through Eve, is present from the beginning and overcomes the first murderer through argumentation.

A Library and the Garden of Eden

In a study of Shaw's use of gardens and libraries, it should not be overlooked that Shaw, in *Back to Methuselah,* not only makes the garden a major component in at least two of his five plays but also uses the library as the sole setting in a third one, *Gospel of the Brothers Barnabas.* Shaw begins with the presentation of a character: *"an impressive-looking gentleman of 50 is seated writing in a well-furnished spacious study.*[53] There is a coherence between man and room, for as Shaw points out, the components of his attire *"combine with the prosperity indicated by his surroundings, and his air of personal distinction, to suggest the clerical dignitary."*[54] Appropriately, he is *"starkly intellectual,"* in that *"the walls are covered with bookshelves."*[55] This is Franklyn Barnabas, an ex-cleric, who is soon joined by his brother Dr. Conrad Barnabas, professor of biology at Jarrowfields University. Shaw gives a detailed description of the rest of the furnishings, which consist of comfortable library chairs on the hearth rug, the writing table, two Chippendale chairs, and a square, upholstered stool. The room reflects the occupiers: breeding, taste, intelligence, deliberateness, and thoughtfulness.

We have previously established that sometimes Shaw combines the garden and library motif in the same play, and even in the same scene; this he does as well in *Gospel of the Brothers Barnabas.* While the ostensible subjects of the play are religion, biology, politics (with the arrival of Burge and Lubin, two politicians), and the gospel of the brothers, which is that humans can extend their length of time to live to three hundred years by merely willing it, the Garden of Eden constitutes a major part of the discussion as well. In fact, as the play moves on, the idea of the garden, Eden included, seems to represent essential matters and a preferred value system. Haslam, the local rector, introduces the subject as he complains that when the bishop makes out-of-date comments, "the bird starts in my garden." "The bird?" queries Franklyn. "Oh yes," Haslam replies. "Theres a bird there that keeps on singing 'Stick it or chuck it: stick it or chuck it'—just like that—for an hour on end in the spring."[56] The garden here is a reflection of the rector's unconscious mind, expressing his internal conflict with the British ecclesiastical establishment. Shortly afterward, Conrad requests that Franklyn's daughter, Savvy, take the rector "into the garden," where he once again may hear the voice of his unconscious and decide to "chuck it." Later, Franklyn contends that if he and his brother, Conrad, have not made religion and biology interesting with their new theories, "we may just as well go out and dig the garden until it is time to dig our graves."[57] The line clearly echoes Adam's statements about "digging in the garden" and reflects the brothers' challenge as theorists. Burge keeps the subject alive by stressing, "I want to cultivate my garden. I am not interested in politics: I am interested in roses," implying that cultivating a flower garden is more valuable than politics.[58] In another discussion when the subject of Karl Marx comes up, Savvy tries to denigrate Marx, saying, "it's like hearing a man talk about the Garden of Eden." But Conrad, the biologist, objects to Savvy's statement and praises the Genesis story: "Why shouldnt he talk about the Garden of Eden? It was a first attempt at biology anyhow." Lubin, also a politician, brags, "I am sound on the Garden of Eden. I have heard of Darwin."[59]

The Garden of Eden begins to assume an important place here in the library. Franklyn, the ex-cleric, takes up the unexpected position that "the poem is our real clue to biological science. The *most scientific document* we possess at present is, as your grandmother would have told you quite truly, *the story of the Garden of Eden*" (emphasis added).[60] After this, Franklyn, Burge, and Lubin engage in a discussion of the issue of Adam, Eve, and mortality. At this point, Shaw is using a discussion in one of his plays, *Gospel of the Brothers Barnabas*, to critique the action of another play, *In the Beginning*, this being perhaps an example of the postmodern quality of self-referentiality. The discussion centers on Adam's and Eve's dilemma of dying by an accidental death or living forever, neither of which they could bear. Finally, the discussion culminates with Savvy stating, "I believe the old people are the new people reincarnated, Nunk. I suspect I am Eve. I am very fond of apples; and they always disagree with me."[61] Conrad explains that Eternal Life "wears out Its bodies and minds and gets new ones, like new clothes. You are only a new hat and frock on Eve."[62] Franklyn makes one last defense of the book of Genesis by talking about the story's persistence and durability, which is a scientific fact, which, if science does not recognize, "then science is more ignorant than the children at any village school."[63] Shaw also picks up on the motif of "thistles" from *In the Beginning,* and we discover why Adam "let the thistles grow": "life was so short that it was no longer worth his while to do anything thoroughly well."[64] Shaw, in *Gospel of the Brothers Barnabas,* again combines gardens and libraries in yet a new way.

Back to the Garden

As Shaw begins to draw near the end of the cycle of *Back to Methuselah,* he also brings everything—setting, characters, motifs, and Lilith—around full circle. It began in a garden with a serpent, Adam and Eve, and a discussion about Lilith; it ends in a garden with a serpent, Adam and Eve, and a discussion by Lilith.

But before Shaw gets to the last play, toward the end of the penultimate play, the serpent motif reappears. At the end of *Tragedy of an Elderly Gentleman,* the Elderly Gentleman, the Envoy, his Wife, and their Daughter, having requested permission to ask the oracle a question, come to the shrine of the oracle. The oracle is referred to as a Pythoness, even though the Elderly Gentleman, as part of Shaw's elusiveness, denies that it is a snake,[65] but the Daughter trembles at the sight of "serpents curling in the vapor."[66] The Pythoness's oracular statement is the brutally realistic, commonsensical advice, "Go home, you fool."[67] After the show is over, the Elderly Gentleman returns to talk to the Pythoness, now in her regular appearance and size. He wishes to be able to stay with her, because he "cannot live among people to whom nothing is real,"[68] even though the Pythoness cautions him that reality will overwhelm him with discouragement, which it does. Why does Shaw present the oracle of reality as a serpent? Is it his way of invoking the story of the Garden of Eden? Is Shaw perhaps saying that the original serpent was the realist, that a state of innocence (as in the Garden of Eden) is an unrealistic fairy tale, and that the truth of the matter is that, realistically, there is good and evil in the world, and human beings will die? The serpent's last words in Shaw's play are,

"I chose wisdom and the knowledge of good and evil; and now there is no evil; and wisdom and good are one. It is enough."[69] Does Shaw view the original serpent also as an oracle of reality—realism, one of Shaw's highest values? Has God been usurped by Lilith? Shaw is certainly going against the Judeo-Christian grain here, which is nothing unusual for him.

In the last play of the cycle, *As Far as Thought Can Reach*, Shaw describes the set as having a *"sunlit glade"* on one side, *"a small little classic temple"* in the middle, and *"a grove"* on the opposite side. This grove, which is technically a garden, provides the locale for the last scene. First appear Eve (which might suggest a predominance of the female), then Adam, Cain, and then the serpent, who *"becomes visible, coiled in the tree,"*[70] as in the opening scene, and introduces Lilith, who speaks of the pain of her creations. After everyone has left the stage, Lilith ruminates on what has been and what could be, with no conclusion about anything. This speech, in Crompton Rhodes's opinion, "for pure thought surpasses in beauty and profundity any words of John Milton";[71] J. C. Squire, who also reviewed the play when it was new, said that it was "conceived finely, and constructed with extraordinary skill."[72] Lilith ponders whether to start a new species ("shall I labor again?").[73] While she is vexed that her creations have done "terrible things," she seems pleased that they are still struggling toward the "goal of redemption,"[74] which means freeing their spirit from matter, which is the enemy of life. She says that the saving quality of the race is "curiosity," the ability to grow and not stagnate. She also sees hope, in that humankind seems to be "reaching out towards" becoming "all life and no matter"; for that she will spare them. She also knows that one day her seed shall "master its matter to its uttermost confines." Beyond that, "it is enough that there is a beyond."[75]

What are the implications of the fact that Lilith, in addition to spawning human life at the beginning, seems to be responsible for making judgments, life-and-death decisions, creating life ("I brought life into the whirlpool of force"),[76] and affecting eternal matters at the end? Again, Shaw has Lilith acting like God; she assumes that if she decides to spare humankind, she has the power to do so: "From the moment I, Lilith, lose hope and faith in them, they are doomed. [. . .] and I may not spare them forever."[77] And, we repeat, where is God in all this? Shaw seems to have replaced God with Lilith. Lilith is a female. A female is in charge of life. Man is at the mercy of a female, and we are reminded of the most persistent aspect of Lilith's legend: seducer, controller, and manipulator of men. We know that Shaw, especially in his earlier years, was extremely reluctant to commit to a relationship with a woman for fear of getting trapped and unable to fulfill his mission as an artist. And in his plays, a man with a noble calling, such as Octavius in *Man and Superman,* among others, must grapple with the threat of being consumed by a woman. As Tanner tells Tavy, "of all human struggles there is none so treacherous and remorseless as the struggle between the artist man and the mother woman."[78] Shaw seems to admit that the female is more powerful than the male, that the female serves the higher purpose of the Life Force, whose purpose is feminine in nature, and that most males are helpless in the face of this awesome power, against which few males may successfully struggle. In other plays, as in *Back to Methuselah,* Shaw seems to concede and admire the superiority of women, and Lilith may be the ultimate portrayal of such superiority, who begins and ends, fittingly, in Shaw's play, in a garden.

Conclusion

Having conducted this close examination of Shaw's use of settings—specifically his use of gardens and libraries—we can safely describe the patterns and significance of those settings. In brief, we may conclude that Shaw incorporates these two settings, which recur with regularity throughout his works, as a way of providing a complete dramatic experience, these settings becoming an extension of the characters, conflicts, and themes as well as a supplement to the language experience of his plays.

The theatre is a listening place, and language tends to dominate drama. Anyone familiar with Shaw's plays knows that one of his great strengths is his use of language, and much of the power that resides in his plays comes from his language. Shaw made no apologies for his talk, calling his plays dramas of discussion, advocating that dramatic values emanate from discussing opposing points of view, and admitting that his plays are all talk, just as Michelangelo's statues are all marble and Beethoven's music is all notes. His plays are largely composed of the clash of ideas, verbal interaction, lengthy conversations, sometimes long speeches, and a lot of talk, brilliant though it may be.

But while Shaw is a verbal genius, his talents go far beyond that. A study of his use of settings leads us to the conclusion that, first, he is also a very visual artist; second, that these settings provide strong performance values; third, these settings serve as metaphors; and fourth, these settings lend insight into his characters.

Visual Effects

The fact that Shaw is an extremely visual playwright may be seen in almost all of his plays, but one play in particular, *Widowers' Houses,* provides an exceptionally poignant example of his use of libraries. We recall that at the beginning of act 2, located in Sartorius's library, Shaw points out in his set description that "all the walls are lined with shelves of smartly tooled books, fitting into their places like bricks." This serves as a visual, ironic counterpoint in several ways in the play. First, Blanche is seen reading, not books from this library, but *The Queen,* which is a tabloidlike paper containing court gossip, and the fact that the books are fitted "into their places like bricks" probably suggests that they are seldom if ever taken off the shelves. Second, like so much else of the hypocrisy in Sartorius's life, this impressive library is there for appearance only, for when Cokane comments on "these books," Sartorius states, "I have not looked into them. They are pleasant for Blanche occasionally when she wishes to read," a statement that is belied by the opening scene with Blanche reading *The Queen.* And third, an even more powerful visual effect is achieved when, toward the end of act 2, and still in the same library, Blanche loses her temper with the parlor maid and seizes *"her by the hair and throat,"* threatens to kill her, and *"tightens"* her fingers *"furiously on her."* The sharp irony here is that the audience, watching a performance, would be aware that Blanche's inhumane behavior is taking place right in front of the *"smartly tooled books,"* the symbol of civilization and culture, both of which she only pretends to but neither of which she is possessed of.

Performance Values

As noted in the introduction, performance theory underlies many of the analyses of scenes occurring in either a garden or a library, and the pursuit of the study of performance values is richly rewarding because, as a study of these settings establishes, Shaw has a keen sense of performativity. While numerous examples of tableaux can be cited throughout Shaw, a very powerful one occurs in *Mrs. Warren's Profession* in act 3, where Vivie and Crofts have a critical discussion about the nature of the businesses run by Crofts and Kitty Warren, and Crofts explains to Vivie how British society works. Vivie seeks to flee the entrapment of the British garden to find freedom and independence in London. As the discussion ends, Vivie goes to the garden gate and *"raises the latch of the gate to open it and go out."* But Crofts *"follows her and puts his hand heavily on the top bar to prevent its opening,"* and this stage picture of Vivie trying to open the gate and Crofts preventing it is a graphic depiction of the conflict of the play, capturing in one picture Vivie's desire for freedom and independence and Mrs. Warren's desire, as represented by Crofts, to keep Vivie with her in order to join respectable members of British society.

Nearly every play by Shaw has examples of his use of tableaux that add to the performance value of the play, but two other striking examples come to mind, *Man and Superman* and *Misalliance,* both of which involve a garden. At the end of *Man and Superman,* in a garden in Granada, several such scenes occur in succession. First, as evidence that Ann Whitefield has finally conquered Tanner, or, in Tanner's words "trapped" him, he seizes her in his arms and "clasps" her, all the while denying that he will marry her; but the physical picture of his holding her outweighs his words, "except when he says 'I have the whole world in my arms when I clasp you." Second, when Ann realizes that Tanner has succumbed, she faints, creating a scene of frenetic activity, briefly rousing herself, and then, in Shaw's words, relapsing with a *"sigh of intense relief."* Ann is then content to lie *"supine"* and announce, "I'm quite happy." Both Ann and Tanner have confessed that they are in the grip of the Life Force, and the picture of Ann lying in a supine position on "mother earth" is symbolic of her connection to the Life Force. Finally, when Ann goes to Octavius to seek congratulations, Tanner says to her, "Ann: stop tempting Tavy, and come back to me." Ann's physical act, then, of leaving Octavius and returning to Tanner is a physical enactment of what has happened in the play by her choosing Tanner over Octavius.

In *Misalliance,* Shaw arranges the set in such a way that there is a glass wall, or *"pavilion"* as he calls it, upstage through which can be seen a *"garden, and, beyond it, a barren but lovely landscape of hill profile with fir trees, commons of bracken and gorse, and wonderful cloud pictures."* This outdoor setting will provide the backdrop for a meaningful scene between Hypatia and Percival. The action between them begins in the pavilion, where Hypatia coaxes Percival to "play on the hill and race through the heather," her aggressiveness eliciting the suggestion of "Potiphar's wife." Percival soon "bolts" through the garden door, while Tarleton, *"looking up at the flying figures with amazement* [. . .] *as they rush away through the garden,"* goes to the door and looks up to nature for an answer, *"but the heavens are empty."* The important stage picture appears when the chase between Hypatia and Percival is reversed and Percival is chasing Hypatia. Hypatia's voice is heard outside, and she *"is seen darting across the garden with Percival in hot pursuit."* She then appears again as she runs into the pavilion followed by

Percival, who rushes in and seizes her until they both realize that they are not alone. Hypatia began the chase, but Percival ends up chasing her, until she catches him—and he is trapped. The sight of Percival chasing Hypatia through nature is Shaw's performance statement of how women, acting under the influence of the Life Force, initiate the pursuit in which the men, whether they wish it or not, become complicit. The scene is appropriately placed in nature, for nature is the underlying force driving both Percival and Hypatia, as suggested when Percival says to Tarleton, "these woods of yours are full of magic" and "the pursuer became the pursued."

Metaphorical Usages

Another conclusion that we can reach is that Shaw uses gardens and library settings as significant metaphors, reminiscent perhaps of Shakespeare's garden scene in *Richard II*:

> Why should we, in the compass of a pale,
> Keep law and form and due proportions,
> Showing as in a model our firm estate,
> When our sea-walled garden, the whole land,
> Is full of weeds, her fairest flowers choked up,
> Her fruit trees all unpruned, her hedges ruined,
> Her knots disordered, and her wholesome herbs
> Swarming with caterpillars? (3.4.43–50)

Shaw uses the garden in several plays as a metaphor for England and English society. In *Widowers' Houses,* even though the garden is a restaurant garden in Germany, the strict rules of English society are enforced, especially by Cokane, who insists on proper appearances ("how are they to know that you are well connected if you do not shew it by your costume?"), common decency ("remember that you are a Gentleman"), formality ("do drop calling me Billy in public"), certain rules and assumptions ("apparently idle ceremonial trifles, really the springs and wheels of a great aristocratic system"), tact ("he's rather an ass in some ways; but he has tremendous tact"), and conservative social rules (Trench says to Blanche, "I beg your pardon for calling you by your name"). In this case, British society is metaphorically extended to a foreign garden, but a garden nevertheless.

In *Mrs. Warren's Profession,* the two different garden settings represent to Vivie the conventionality, respectability, and parental authoritarianism, as practiced by her mother, Kitty Warren, from which she seeks, as the main plotline of the play, to break free and go her own independent way. The British garden represents the repression of British society to the freedom-seeking Vivie.

Other metaphorical usages of the garden also occur. In *Heartbreak House,* the setting of Captain Shotover's house symbolizes the English "ship of state," the last scene of which takes place in the garden. The metaphorical overtones of the garden are articulated when the captain advises everyone to "think of this garden in which you are not a dog barking to keep the truth out," implying that the garden is a place of truth and the humans are not like dogs, vainly barking to keep the truth out. The garden becomes a place of truth, as when Mangan says, as he begins to strip off his clothes, "let's all strip stark naked" because "we've stripped ourselves morally naked as well." Mangan's action is a metaphorical expression of what is occurring in the metaphorical garden of truth.

Character Revelation

Finally, Shaw uses the garden and library settings as a another way of revealing characters visually, going beyond the mere detailed descriptions he gives of them in his stage directions and providing insight into various aspects of their makeup. As noted earlier, Carl Jung theorizes that the place one inhabits is an extension of the self and renders insights into the occupant. Shaw does this with gardens and libraries in a number of his plays, among them *Arms and the Man, Candida,* and *Major Barbara.*

Shaw describes the garden setting in *Arms and the Man* as *"fresh and pretty. Beyond the paling the tops of a couple of minarets can be seen, shewing that there is a valley there, with the little town in it."* The Petkoffs literally live high above the rest of the village, and of course they see themselves as being above other Bulgarians with their pretense to aristocracy. Shaw continues: *"A few miles further the Balkan mountains rise and shut in the landscape."* Like the rest of Bulgaria, the Petkoffs are isolated, alienated from the rest of the world, which leads to their insularity, lack of sophistication, and provincialism. Shaw adds depth to the whole character revelation by noting that the stable yard encroaches on the garden and that the *"fruit bushes along the paling and house* [are] *covered with washing spread out to dry."* These descriptions undercut all the aristocratic pretenses of the Petkoffs: rather than a garden for sipping tea and enjoying social intercourse, it reeks of the stable yard, as well as the workaday world, which encroaches into it, and the sight of the laundry drying on the bushes symbolizes the fact that the owners know little about gardens as status symbols. Petkoff himself tells his wife that "civilized people dont hang out their washing to dry where visitors can see it; so youd better have all that [*indicating the clothes on the bushes*] put somewhere else."

In *Candida,* in spite of the title, the setting belongs to the Reverend James Mavor Morell, for the onstage setting is located in his library and the immediate offstage setting is the 217 acres of Victoria Park, the best view of which, according to Shaw, is from the parson's window. His library reflects his concern with social issues, his location in East End London makes his message of progressive thought popular, and his 217-acre garden, stretching out from his window, symbolizes his self-centeredness.

The setting in act 1 of *Major Barbara* is the library in Lady Britomart Undershaft's house in Wilton Crescent. As a member of the "upper class," as Shaw points out, everything for her must show good breeding, correctness, and the right appearance, *"being quite enlightened and liberal as to the books in the library, the pictures on the walls, the music in the portfolios, and the articles in the papers."* The room is symbolic of Lady Britomart's determination to convey the right image of upper-class advanced thinking.

While a study of Shaw's use of gardens and libraries is a rather limited, focused study of Shaw's use of settings, it does portray Shaw as going beyond mere language for his dramatic affects and reveals other dimensions of Shaw's dramaturgy, such as his visual acumen, his sense of performance values, his use of setting as metaphor, and his revelation of characters through settings, showing him to be the complete playwright.

NOTES

Introduction

1. Rodelle Weintraub, "Johnny's Dream in *Misalliance*," 179.
2. Arthur Ganz, *George Bernard Shaw*, 54.
3. George Bernard Shaw, *Widowers' Houses*, in *Plays Unpleasant: Widowers' Houses; The Philanderer; Mrs Warren's Profession*, 31. Future citations are from this edition.
4. Ibid., 53.
5. Michael Holroyd, *Bernard Shaw: The One-Volume Definitive Edition*, 51.
6. Ibid.
7. Caryl Churchill, *Serious Money*, 230–31.
8. Richard Schechner, *Performance Studies: An Introduction*, 2.
9. Raymond Williams, *Drama in Performance*, 4.
10. Ibid.
11. Ibid., 4–5.
12. Ibid., 172–73.
13. Ibid., 178.
14. Ibid., 177.
15. Ibid., 189.

Chapter 1. *Widowers' Houses*: "Life Here Is a Perfect Idyll"

1. Frederick J. Marker, "Shaw's Early Play," 110.
2. Ganz, *Shaw*, 81.
3. Frederick P. W. McDowell, "*Widowers' Houses*: A Play for the 1890s and the 1990s," 231.
4. Ibid., 239.
5. Ibid., 238.
6. Ibid.
7. Charles Carpenter, *Bernard Shaw and the Art of Destroying Ideals: The Early Plays*. 35.
8. Ibid., 36.

9. Marker, "Shaw's Early Play," 104.

10. Carpenter, *Shaw and the Art of Destroying Ideals*, 40.

11. Ganz, *Shaw*, 85.

12. Marker, "Shaw's Early Play," 106.

13. Kristin Morrison, "Horrible Flesh and Blood," 8.

14. Morrison quotes from a letter from Wilde to Shaw about his reading of and admiration for *Widowers' Houses*, "with its detailed character descriptions," after which "Wilde for the first time used such descriptions in a play of his own," and "they sound just like Shaw's" (ibid., 8). The play under discussion is *An Ideal Husband*, which, according to Morrison, "abounds in this [the description of Lickcheese] kind of Shavian detail for both major and minor characters," and, she continues, "these interpretive stage directions represent the influence of Shaw" (9). Before Wilde's encounter with *Widowers' Houses*, this was not Wilde's "custom" (7).

15. Shaw, *Widowers' Houses*, 31.

16. Ibid., 32.

17. Ibid.

18. Ibid., 33.

19. Ibid., 32.

20. Ibid., 42.

21. Ibid., 34.

22. Ibid., 35.

23. Ibid., 42.

24. Ibid.

25. Ibid., 47.

26. McDowell, *"Widowers' Houses,"* 238.

27. James Woodfield, "Shaw's *Widowers' Houses*: Comedy for Socialism's Sake," 55.

28. Shaw, *Widowers' Houses*, 27.

29. Ibid., 33.

30. Ibid.

31. Ibid.

32. Ibid., 34.

33. Ibid., 37.

34. Ibid., 33.

35. Ibid., 44.

36. Ibid.

37. Ibid.

38. Ibid.

39. Ganz, *Shaw*, 81.

40. Woodfield, "Shaw's *Widowers' Houses*," 56.

41. Shaw, *Widowers' Houses*, 50.

42. Ibid., 52.

43. Ibid., 37.

44. Ibid., 38.

45. Ibid., 44.

46. Ibid.

47. Ibid., 38.

48. Ibid., 39.

49. Ibid.

50. Ibid., 41.

51. McDowell, *"Widowers' Houses,"* 238.

52. Woodfield, "Shaw's *Widowers' Houses,"* 54.

53. Martha Vogeler, *"Widowers' Houses* and the London County Council," 5.

54. Shaw, *Widower's Houses,* 57.

55. Ibid., 60. Raymond S. Nelson, in "Shaw's *Widowers' Houses,"* 27–37, quotes from Reverend Andrew Mearns's *The Bitter Cry of Outcast Land,* which is quoted in J. A. R. Pimlott, *Toynbee Hall: Fifty Years of Social Progress, 1884–1934* (London, 1935), 30. Talking about a slum he visited, Mearns wrote, "to get into them you have to penetrate courts reeking with poisonous and malodorous gases arising from accumulations of sewage and refuse scattered in all directions and often flowing beneath your feet; courts many of them which the sun never penetrates and which are never visited by a breath of air. Drains and sewers were bad if they existed, and most tenements like those in Robbins's Row had poor drainage and high death rates"; Nelson adds, "Shaw knew these conditions well" ("Shaw's *Widowers' Houses,"* 32).

56. Shaw, *Widowers' Houses,* 36.

57. Ibid.

58. Ibid., 60.

59. Ibid., 61.

60. Ibid., 62.

61. Ibid., 58.

62. Ibid., 61.

63. Ibid. McDowell notes that Blanche's "indifference toward the unfortunate, her possessiveness, and her cruelty are not only personal qualities, they are also symbolic of a demoralized, unjust society" (*"Widowers' Houses,"* 237).

64. Shaw, *Widowers' Houses,* 53.

65. Ibid.

66. Marker, "Shaw's Early Play," 108.

67. Shaw, *Widowers' Houses,* 57.

68. Ibid., 53.

69. Ibid., 54.

70. Ibid., 64.

71. Ibid., 65.

72. Ibid., 66.

73. Ibid., 67.

74. Ibid., 78.

75. Bernard Dukore, *"Widowers' Houses:* A Question of Genre," 31.

76. Ibid.

77. Shaw, *Widowers' Houses,* 78.

78. Ibid., 85.

79. Ibid., 82.
80. Ibid., 85.
81. Ibid., 86.
82. Ibid.
83. Ibid., 87.
84. Ibid., 88.

Chapter 2. *Mrs. Warren's Profession*: The Walled Gardens

1. Alan S. Downer, introduction to George Bernard Shaw, *The Theatre of Bernard Shaw*, 21.

2. Carpenter, *Shaw and the Art of Destroying Ideals*, 52–53.

3. Dan H. Laurence, "Victorians Unveiled: Some Thoughts on *Mrs. Warren's Profession*," 40.

4. Ibid., 41–42.

5. Ibid., 44.

6. Ganz, *Shaw*, 93–94.

7. Downer, introduction to Shaw, *Theatre of Bernard Shaw*, 21.

8. Laurence, "Victorians Unveiled," 42.

9. George Bernard Shaw, *Mrs. Warren's Profession*, in *Plays Unpleasant*, 213. Future citations are from this edition.

10. Ibid.

11. Peter Mudford, after quoting Tolstoy on the horrors of the profession of prostitution, makes the point that it is an "unsavory profession" (*"Mrs. Warren's Profession*," 6). He points out that Shaw completely avoids that aspect of prostitution and remarks on the "fastidiousness with which the whole play is conceived." After labeling it as a "disinfected approach," Mudford comments, "it would be hard to imagine a play about prostitution more completely empty of its crude physicality—of the shadows of violence and disease" and suggests that Shaw removes "his characters a good distance from their usual lives" by sending them to Haslemere—rural, outdoors, agrarian, and close to nature (8). Mudford's observation can be taken one step further by noting how Shaw sharpens the irony of the whole situation, especially that of Kitty Warren and George Crofts, who run the day-to-day operations of their nasty business, by placing them in a pleasant English garden on an idyllic afternoon, removing them even further from their "unsavory profession."

12. Shaw, *Mrs. Warren's Profession*, 252.

13. Ibid., 253.

14. Ibid.

15. Ibid.

16. Ibid., 256.

17. Ibid., 251.

18. Ibid., 265.

19. Ibid.

20. Ibid.

21. Ibid.

22. Ibid., 266.

23. Ibid., 268.

24. Ibid., 231.

25. Ganz, *Shaw*, 93.

26. Mudford, "*Mrs. Warren's Profession*," 9.

27. Calvin T. Higgs Jr., "Shaw's Use of Vergil's *Aeneid* in *Arms and the Man*," 2.

28. Shaw, *Mrs. Warren's Profession*, 231.

29. Ibid., 216.

30. Ibid., 267.

31. Ibid., 277.

32. Carpenter, *Shaw and the Art of Destroying Ideals*, 52.

33. Shaw, *Mrs. Warren's Profession*, 227.

34. Ibid., 230.

35. Ibid., 283.

36. Ibid., 261.

37. Ibid., 264.

38. Ibid.

39. Ibid., 265.

40. Ibid.

41. Ibid., 249.

42. Ibid., 251.

43. Ibid., 257.

44. Ibid.

45. Ibid., 283.

46. Ibid., 258.

47. Ibid., 285.

48. Ibid., 286.

49. Ibid.

50. Ibid.

51. Ibid., 245.

52. While no one argues that Vivie is the picture of perfection, with her many limitations showing clearly (her abnormal rudeness toward her mother being one), scholars have given many reasons to admire her as a dramatic character. Marie Parker Wasserman praises Shaw for creating a psychological study in Vivie and going beyond mere literary type. She also adds that Vivie's portrayal is a "psychological one, probing Vivie as a living woman, not just typing Vivie as a liberated woman" ("Vivie Warren: A Psychological Study," 168). Leonard Conolly investigated Cambridge University's situation when Vivie would have been there, demonstrating that Vivie would have studied in "a largely inhospitable academic environment for women" ("Who Was Phillipa Summers? Reflections on Vivie Warren's Cambridge," 93). Conolly concludes that Vivie needed "extraordinary commitment and single-mindedness" to survive Cambridge and that she would need those "attributes even more to establish herself and to prosper in the professional world she enters after leaving Cambridge—a world dominated, like Cambridge, by men" (94).

53. Ganz, *Shaw,* 98.

54. Carpenter, *Shaw and the Art of Destroying Ideals,* 7. This was a comment made by Shaw at a debate and paraphrased by Stephen Winsten, *Jesting Apostle: The Life of Bernard Shaw,* 71.

Chapter 3. *Arms and the Man*: "I Took Care to Let Them Know That We Have a Library"

1. "Realism" in this chapter refers primarily to surface verisimilitude rather than the reality of the inner essence of things, the inner "reality" of Plato, Shelley, and Ibsen that Shaw develops in *The Quintessence of Ibsenism.* Shaw's use of the word *realism* was always problematical in that he had two different, almost opposite usages in mind.

2. Lawrence Perrine, "Shaw's *Arms and the Man,*" 5.

3. Carpenter, *Shaw and the Art of Destroying Ideals,* 88.

4. Ganz, *Shaw,* 100.

5. Ibid., 99.

6. Louis Crompton, introduction to *Arms and the Man,* xxiii.

7. Charles Berst, "Romance and Reality in *Arms and the Man,*" 201.

8. Ibid., 199.

9. Ibid., 211.

10. Bernard Dukore, "The Ablest Man in Bulgaria," 68.

11. Samuel Weiss, "Shaw, *Arms and the Man,* and the Bulgarians," 28.

12. Ibid.

13. Ibid., 29.

14. Ibid., 38.

15. Ibid., 39.

16. Ibid.

17. Ibid.

18. Roumiana Deltcheva, "East Central Europe as a Politically Correct Scapegoat: The Case of Bulgaria," 7.

19. Crompton, introduction, xvi.

20. Edward Dicey, *The Peasant State: An Account of Bulgaria in 1894,* 55.

21. Shaw, *Shaw on Theatre,* 23.

22. Weiss, "Shaw, *Arms and the Man,* and the Bulgarians," 37.

23. Ibid.

24. No doubt Shaw's honest depiction of the Bulgarians has cost him some criticism, such as Deltcheva's declaration that *Arms* is "a prime example of the British condescending, imperialist attitude towards the European margins" ("East Central Europe," 6), but the truth is that Shaw is merely being faithful to history and the facts.

25. Berst, "Romance and Reality," 210.

26. Shaw, *Arms and the Man,* 119.

27. Dukore, "Ablest Man," 72.

28. George Bernard Shaw, *Arms and the Man,* 119.

29. Ibid., 121.

30. Ibid., 122.

31. Ibid.

32. Deltcheva contends that Shaw, through the Petkoffs, has marginalized the Bulgarians and portrays Petkoff as "not only . . . ignorant, pretentious, and ridiculous, [but] also uncleanly and mocks people who wash every day" ("East Central Europe," 8). Deltcheva confuses Shaw's historical accuracy and objectivity with viciousness on his part.

33. Shaw, *Arms and the Man*, 114–15.

34. Weiss points out that in spite of the fact that Bulgaria was a backward nation with "peasant living conditions," "in time the bourgeoisie revived Bulgarian architecture, two or three story homes, thick walls" and "lush gardens" ("Shaw, *Arms and the Man*, and the Bulgarians," 37). The Petkoffs are merely in the vanguard of leading their country out of its peasant condition, and Shaw has captured the bifurcated nature of a family in transition.

35. Shaw, *Arms and the Man*, 115.

36. Carpenter, *Shaw and the Art of Destroying Ideals*, 91.

37. Shaw, *Arms and the Man*, 113.

38. Ibid., 134. When Deltcheva uses the scene as proof that Shaw is making fun of Bulgarians because the Westerner (Bluntschli) is "simply incredulous" that the Petkoffs would have a library ("East Central Europe," 7), she completely misses Bluntschli's playful tone. In fact, all through the scene, Bluntschli, being tired and possibly in grave danger, politely pretends to be impressed with what Raina is telling him about her family, to the point that she even scolds him at one point with, "how can you stoop to pretend" (115). His reaction to the library is in keeping with his other responses. Weiss takes a more sober attitude toward the library, acknowledging that it represents "the arrival of western civilization in the Balkans" ("Shaw, *Arms and the Man*, and the Bulgarians," 37).

39. Shaw, *Arms and the Man*, 134.

40. Ibid.

41. Ibid.

42. Ibid., 139.

43. Ibid.

44. Ibid., 142. Deltcheva's response to Shaw's description of the library is to label it a "patronizing attitude," that the library is "clearly a Western transplant" that has been "vandalized by the local lack of culture" ("East Central Europe," 7). Shaw's description of *"novels, broken backed, coffee stained, torn and thumbed"* to Deltcheva are "clear markers of a barbaric approach to culture" (7). This is not Shaw's intent; his point is that the books are cheap, paperback, popular romantic novels of the time and thus expose the Petkoffs' pretentiousness to having a library.

45. Shaw, *Arms and the Man*, 142.

46. Ibid., 146.

47. Ibid., 148.

48. Ibid., 155.

49. Ibid., 156.

50. Ibid., 159.

51. Ibid.
52. Ibid.
53. David K. Sauer, "'Only a Woman' in *Arms and the Man*," 162.
54. Shaw, *Arms and the Man*, 129.
55. Ibid., 166.
56. Ibid., 129.
57. Ibid., 101.
58. Ibid., 100.
59. Ibid., 101.
60. Ibid., 129.
61. Ibid., 142.
62. Ibid.
63. Ibid., 153.
64. Ibid., 101.
65. Ibid., 124.
66. Ibid., 125.
67. Ibid.
68. Ibid., 103.
69. Ibid., 123.
70. Ibid.
71. Ibid.
72. Ibid., 119.
73. Ibid.
74. Ibid.
75. Ibid.
76. Weiss, "Shaw, *Arms and the Man,* and the Bulgarians," 37.
77. Berst, "Romance and Reality," 209.
78. Shaw, *Arms and the Man*, 129.
79. Ibid., 130.
80. Ibid., 132. Berst points out that "the strain of higher love is too great because it has no meaningful contact with the true personalities of either" party "because it "involves the mere acting of a foreign role" ("Romance and Reality," 206). Sergius's attraction to Louka is not, as Deltcheva argues, because he is a "sex maniac" ("East Central Europe," 7), but is based on refreshingly honest feelings. Perrine suggests that Sergius remains an "unchanged and a confirmed romanticist to the end," but the truth is that Sergius has many of his delusions completely shattered in the garden and in the library ("Shaw's *Arms and the Man*," 6).
81. Shaw, *Arms and the Man*, 132.
82. Ibid., 135.
83. Ibid., 131.

Chapter 4. *Candida*: A Wall of Bookshelves and the Best View of the Garden

1. Ganz, *Shaw*, 104.
2. James Woodfield, "Shaw's *Candida*: A Comedy," 445.

3. Walter N. King, "The Rhetoric of *Candida*," 71.

4. Arthur H. Nethercot, "The Truth about *Candida*," 639.

5. Charles Berst, "The Craft of *Candida*," 158.

6. Ibid., 162.

7. Ibid., 161.

8. Woodfield, "Shaw's *Candida*," 450.

9. Ibid., 435.

10. Walter Lazenby, "Love and 'Vitality' in *Candida*," 18.

11. Jacob H. Adler, "Ibsen, Shaw, and *Candida*," 51.

12. William J. Doan, "*Candida*: The Eye on Duty," 135.

13. King, "Rhetoric of *Candida*," 71.

14. Berst, "Craft of *Candida*," 160.

15. Ibid., 169.

16. Ibid.

17. Ibid., 165.

18. Elsie Adams, "Bernard Shaw's Pre-Raphaelite Drama," 435.

19. Carpenter, *Shaw and the Art of Destroying Ideals*, 116.

20. Harold Pagliaro, "Truncated Love in *Candida* and *Heartbreak House*," 208.

21. John Lucas, "Dickens and Shaw: Women and Marriage in *David Copperfield* and *Candida*," 17.

22. Patrick White, "*Candida*: Bernard Shaw's Chaucerian Drama," 218.

23. Herbert Bergman, "The Comedy in *Candida*," 161.

24. George Bernard Shaw, *Collected Letters*, vol. 2, *1898–1910*, 396.

25. Lazenby, "Love and 'Vitality,'" 11.

26. Pagliaro, "Truncated Love," 205.

27. George Bernard Shaw, *Candida*, in *Plays Pleasant: Arms and the Man; Candida; The Man of Destiny; You Never Can Tell*, 93. Future citations are from this edition.

28. Ibid.

29. Ibid.

30. Ibid.

31. Ibid.

32. Ibid.

33. Ibid.

34. Ibid.

35. Ibid., 39.

36. Ibid., 40.

37. Ibid.

38. Ibid., 95.

39. "Stewart Headlam."

40. Shaw, *Candida*, 94.

41. Ibid.

42. Ibid.

43. Ibid.

44. Ibid.

45. Ibid.

46. Ibid.

47. Ibid., 100.

48. Ibid.

49. While it may be true that Candida is in part responsible for the arrangement of the room—*"the room of a good housekeeper"* who is *"mistress of the situation"*—the room would then also reflect her view of him, so the room would still mirror certain aspects of his personality. It should also be noted that on the wall hangs a *"large autotype of the chief figure in Titian's Assumption of the Virgin."* This seems to be an extraneous item in the room, for it is Marchbanks who is responsible, as we later discover, for its being there. As Shaw says, *"whoever had placed"* it there did so because he *"fancied some spiritual resemblance between"* the Virgin and Candida, of which, as Shaw says, Candida and Morell are unaware. Thus, the painting makes no statement about Morell, but it does about Marchbanks.

50. Shaw, *Candida*, 94.

51. Ibid.

52. One cannot help but feel that Shaw is critiquing and possibly adding a cautionary note to Morell's socialist beliefs. Many of the Christian Socialists of his day believed that through a combination of Christianity and social and economic equality they could establish a heaven on earth, just as Morell talks about, as when he tells Marchbanks that it is nothing but human folly that keeps the world from being a paradise. Charles Carpenter points out, "this is the Marxian apocalyptic view of socialism, the view that Shaw opposed in the *Fabian Essays*, in articles on Marx, and in a brief paper written in 1894, the year he began *Candida*" (*Shaw and the Art of Destroying Ideals*, 101). Carpenter notes that Shaw argued in several venues that Social Democracy would by no means bring about the millennium (101). Morell also "assumes that happiness is the proper goal of mankind," as Carpenter points out, and we know Shaw believed that happiness was not the purpose of life (104). While Morell's library reflects Shaw's own taste in social theory, Morell presents a cautionary message about idealism.

53. Shaw, *Candida*, 95.

54. Ibid., 96.

55. Ibid.

56. Ibid., 133.

57. Ibid.

58. Ibid., 135.

59. Ibid., 128.

60. Ibid., 135.

61. Ibid.

62. Ibid., 136.

63. Ibid., 148.

64. Ibid.

65. Ibid., 158.

66. Ibid., 157.

67. Ibid., 95.

68. Ibid., 144.

Chapter 5. *Man and Superman*: Books on a Garden Table

1. George Bernard Shaw, *Man and Superman,* in *The Theatre of Bernard Shaw,* 1: 290. Future citations are from this edition.

2. Ibid.

3. Ibid.

4. Ibid.

5. The only other study of Ramsden's library, it seems, is V. J. Emmett, "Roebuck Ramsden's Study: Shaw as Philosophical Conservative." This article appears to assert several unsupportable assumptions. First it assumes that Ramsden's study reflects Shaw's thinking, when in fact the study is an extension of Ramsden, not Shaw (although Shaw does create the study to reflect Ramsden): "From the list of Victorians memorialized in Ramsden's study, we can see what it is that Shaw does object to" (104)—a specious leap in logic. Second, any personages portrayed in Ramsden's study who do not fit into Emmett's argument are disregarded: Bright and Cobden "need not concern us here" (104), nor does he concern himself with Watts, Dupont, and Delaroche. The present study attempts to include every single item mentioned in Shaw's stage description as conveying important information about Ramsden. Third, Emmett concludes that Shaw, not Ramsden, was "a clever philosophical conservative posing as a radical" (103), that Shaw follows Carlyle rather than Nietzsche (107), and that Shaw's description is a "piece of polemical sleight of hand whereby the relatively new-fangled is made to seem the relatively old-fashion" (108), to Ramsden, not to Shaw.

6. Shaw's selection of the two names, "Roebuck" and "Ramsden," give great insight into Shaw's attitude toward his character. The historical personage, John Roebuck (1718–1794), started his political career promoting a wide range of radical policies, including the expropriation of the property of the Church of England, the repeal of the Corn Laws, and the removal of a tax on newspapers. As time went on, however, he became less extreme and upset his radical friends by losing interest in domestic reform. As he became "increasingly conservative," he stated, "the hopes of my youth and manhood are destroyed and I am left to reconstruct my political philosophy" ("John Roebuck").

Although he had supported universal suffrage during the debate on the 1867 Reform Act, he cautioned against placing political power "in the hands of the ignorant." Eventually, although he had earlier supported the Chartist movement, he denounced the "activities of the trade unionists," and, what must have been particularly galling to Shaw, he opposed William Gladstone's effort to disestablish the Anglican Church in Ireland. In his last elected office, he ran as a member of the Conservative Party (ibid.). It sounds as though Shaw has made Roebuck's namesake character a direct descendent of the original, someone with enlightened pretenses who in reality is an antireformer and conservative at heart.

As for the name Ramsden, aside from its nice alliterative association with Roebuck, Shaw may have had in mind one Jesse Ramsden, the most well-known and historically prominent possessor of that name. Jesse Ramsden (1735–1800) was probably the best manufacturer of scientific instruments of the eighteenth century and well known throughout Europe. His most important and widely used invention was the circular dividing engine, an instrument that had a profound impact on Western history. While the division and inscription of scales on mathematical instruments had been done by hand with an accuracy of no better than three seconds of arc, Ramsden's invention increased the accuracy to a single second, eliminating human error and increasing the production of precise scientific and mathematical instruments. This was particularly important for the development of the octant and the sextant, both vital to the British navy and thus British exploration of the world's oceans and the establishment of the British Empire ("Jesse Ramsden"). Shaw's Ramsden is a moral and social precisionist, quibbling over his positions in exacting ways. In his lecture to Octavius, Ramsden insists that "there are *limits* to social toleration," and "I *draw the line* at Anarchism and Free Love and that sort of thing" (294); he also tells Tanner, "you have got me in a cleft stick" (298)—all positions stated in precise physical terms.

7. Marjorie Bloy, "John Bright (1811–1889)."

8. "Herbert Spencer."

9. Marjorie Bloy, "Richard Cobden (1804–1865)."

10. Valerie Kossew Pichanick, *Harriet Martineau: The Woman and Her work, 1802–76*, 170, 22.

11. Ibid., 49.

12. Ibid.

13. "Thomas Henry Huxley (1825–1895)."

14. "George Eliot: Biography: From Mary Anne Evans to George Eliot."

15. Fiona MacCarthy, "England's Michelangelo."

16. Shaw, *Man and Superman*, 290.

17. MacCarthy, "England's Michelangelo."

18. "Hippolyte Delaroche."

19. Shaw, *Man and Superman*, 293.

20. Ibid.

21. Ibid., 294.

22. Ibid.

23. Ibid., 297.

24. Ibid., 299.

25. Ibid.

26. Ibid.

27. Ibid., 305.

28. Ibid.

29. Ibid.

30. Ibid., 306.

31. Ibid.

32. Ibid.

33. Ibid., 310.

34. Ibid., 334.

35. Ibid.

36. Ibid.

37. José Ortega y Gasset, *The Revolt of the Masses,* 89.

38. Shaw, *Man and Superman,* 338.

39. Ibid., 336.

40. Ibid., 337.

41. Ibid.

42. Ibid.

43. Ibid.

44. Shaw appears to have a comfortable relationship with technology. Not only upon first arriving in London was his first job arranging telephone installations for the Edison Telephone Company, he utilizes technology on stage in a number of plays. In addition to the automobile in *Man and Superman,* he uses the typewriter, a fairly new invention, in *Candida;* he refers to the bulletproof motorcar, the aerial battleship, and the ten-inch gun in *Major Barbara;* he crashes an "aeroplane" into the glass pavilion in *Misalliance;* he uses the zeppelin to drop bombs on *Heartbreak House,* and he utilizes various kinds of devices such as the klaxon electric horn and the "motor bicycle" in *Too True to Be Good.*

45. Shaw, *Man and Superman,* 338.

46. Ibid.

47. Ibid., 342.

48. Ibid., 343.

49. Ibid.

50. Ibid., 354.

51. Ibid., 355.

52. Ibid., 356.

53. Leo Marx, *The Machine in the Garden: Technology and the Pastoral Ideal in America,* 15.

54. Ibid., 16.

55. Ibid., 102–5.

56. Ibid., 15.

57. Ibid., 16.

58. Ibid.

59. Ibid., 27.

60. Shaw, *Man and Superman,* 335.

61. Ibid.

62. Ibid., 336.

63. Ibid.

64. Ibid., 342.

65. Ibid., 346.

66. Ibid., 347.

67. Ibid.

68. Ibid., 356.

69. Ibid., 357.

70. Sally Peters Vogt, in "Ann and Superman: Type and Archetype," notes the significance of this setting as well, suggesting that "act 3 moves toward spatial freedom,

opening in the uncertain light of evening and therefore signaling uncertain space amid the inhospitable arid landscape of the Sierra Nevadas. Scattered patches of olive trees [...] impart an ancient and religious aura. The mountains dominate the action; Tanner refers to the 'august hills,' and much stage movement involves climbing or sitting on rock formations" (119).

71. Shaw, *Man and Superman*, 365.

72. Interestingly, Shaw himself owned a number of automobiles and enjoyed nothing more than touring far and wide in his car, with a chauffeur at the steering wheel.

73. Shaw, *Man and Superman*, 427.

74. For an excellent consideration of the significance of the Alhambra in this scene, see Vogt, "Ann and Superman," 120.

75. Shaw, *Man and Superman*, 427. Vogt has a different interpretation of this garden setting. She says that "this extremely ordered landscape signals the return to the rational, conscious world, while the steps symbolize the spiritual evolution Tanner has achieved." She does say, however, that the "implicit greenness of vegetation and water supports the suggestion of fertility and the life process" ("Ann and Superman," 121), which is in accord with the present reading.

76. Shaw, *Man and Superman*, 427–28.

77. Ibid., 428.

78. Northrop Frye, *Words with Power: Being a Second Study of "The Bible and Literature,"* 201.

79. Ibid., 202.

80. Ibid., 206.

81. For another extensive study of Shaw's use of myth and archetypes, see Vogt, "Ann and Superman."

82. J. L. Wisenthal quotes Shaw's own words in the note that Shaw wrote for the first production of the hell scene (printed in Raymond Mander and Joe Mitchenson, *Theatrical Companion to Shaw* [London: Rockliff, 1954]), that Dona Ana "is done with the bearing of men to mortal fathers, she may yet, as Woman Immortal, bear the Superman to the Eternal Father" (90). Wisenthal explains that by "Woman Immortal" and "the Eternal Father" "Shaw means simply Woman and Man." In trying to explain Shaw's cosmology, Wisenthal connects this to a scene in *Back to Methuselah*, when Savvy says, "I believe the old people are the new people reincarnated, Nunk, I suspect that I am Eve. I am very fond of apples [...] Conrad. You are Eve, in a sense. The Eternal Life persists; only It wears out Its bodies and minds and gets new ones, like new clothes. You are only a new hat and frock on Eve" ("The Cosmology of *Man and Superman*," 304).

83. Frye, drawing on biblical accounts and Plato's *Symposium*, talks about the ladder of love and beauty between this and a higher world, of an ascent and descent from a higher world through love and on which angels are ascending and descending. This metaphor goes on to speak of a "fall or descent into a lower world of morality and sexual self-consciousness," which is what eventually happens to Ann and Tanner (*Words with Power*, 208). Frye cites Plato's *Symposium*, as well as the story of Jacob's ladder, as having a ladder of love accompanied by ascending and descending angels.

84. Shaw, *Man and Superman*, 427.

85. Frye, *Words with Power*, 209.
86. Shaw, *Man and Superman*, 431.
87. Ibid., 430.
88. See Tony J. Stafford, "*Mrs Warren's Profession:* In the Garden of Respectability."
89. Shaw, *Man and Superman*, 433.
90. Ibid.
91. Ibid.
92. Ibid., 434.
93. Ibid., 435.
94. Ibid., 437.
95. Frye, *Words with Power*, 198.
96. Ibid., 195.
97. Ibid., 198.
98. Ibid., 196.
99. Ibid., 199.
100. Vogt suggests that Ann is associated with the female symbol, the moon, while Tanner is linked to the male symbol, the sun ("Ann and Superman," 115, 117). Her summary of them as "world-embracing goddess-mother and the world-renouncing hero-saint" could easily be extended to include Frye's notion of woman as earth and man as sky.
101. Shaw, *Man and Superman*, 302.
102. Ibid., 452.
103. Ibid., 453.
104. Ibid., 455.
105. Ibid.
106. Shaw himself says, "every woman is not Ann; but Ann is Everywoman" (Epistle Dedicatory). Vogt contends that Ann "is archetypal Woman, whose role subsumes all roles. Biologically she may serve the species and socially she may seem to serve men, but psychologically she is free to woo and win as she chooses. [. . .] Paradoxically identified with both the origin of life and the end toward which life aspires, Ann is a culminant figure, epitomizing an entire spectrum of related qualities and exemplifying Shaw's art of dramatic imitation in all the richness of its symbolizing and universalizing aspects" ("Ann and Superman," 122–23).
107. Frye, *Words with Power*, 199.
108. Shaw, *Man and Superman*, 458.
109. Ibid., 302.
110. Ibid., 457.

Chapter 6. *Major Barbara*: The Salvation Army's "Garden" and Cusins's Books

1. Eric Bentley, *Bernard Shaw*, 5.
2. Alfred Turco Jr., *Shaw's Moral Vision: The Self and Salvation*, 193.
3. Robert J. Jordan, "Theme and Character in *Major Barbara*," 473.
4. Michiyo Ishii, "Two Political Implications of Shaw's *Major Barbara*," 23.
5. J. L. Wisenthal, "The Marriage of Contraries: *Major Barbara*," 192.

6. T. J. Matheson, "The Lure of Power and Triumph of Capital: An Ironic Reading of *Major Barbara*," 287.

7. Jordan, "Theme and Character," 473.

8. George Bernard Shaw, preface to *Major Barbara*, in *The Complete Prefaces of Bernard Shaw*, 122.

9. Wisenthal, "Marriage of Contraries," 192.

10. Shaw, preface to *Major Barbara*, 118.

11. Ibid., 122.

12. George Bernard Shaw, *Major Barbara*, in *Bernard Shaw's Plays: Major Barbara; Heartbreak House; Saint Joan; Too True to Be Good*, 65. Future citations are from this edition.

13. Shaw, preface to *Major Barbara*, 122.

14. Ibid.

15. Ibid., 120.

16. Ibid., 124.

17. Wisenthal, "Marriage of Contraries," 189.

18. Bentley, *Shaw*, 17.

19. Larry Herold, "Writing Was Only Step One: Bernard Shaw's Immersion in the Premiere of *Major Barbara*," 37.

20. Shaw, preface to *Major Barbara*, 122.

21. Louis Crompton, *Shaw the Dramatist*, 2.

22. Shaw, *Major Barbara*, 18.

23. Ibid.

24. Ibid.

25. Ibid.

26. Crompton, *Shaw the Dramatist*, 111.

27. Ibid.

28. Shaw, *Major Barbara*, 21.

29. Ibid., 36.

30. Ibid., 34.

31. Critics, as well as Undershaft, make much of Barbara's desire to be a saver of souls, that she is seeking to live her life for some higher purpose, but the truth is that she cuts and runs at the first sign of harsh reality or disappointment. One has to wonder just how dedicated she really is to saving souls. She seems more like a naive idealist than a Shavian hero.

32. Shaw, *Major Barbara*, 56.

33. Act 3 begins *"the next day,"* but Shaw gives no information as to how much time has elapsed in the movement from Wilton Crest to Perivale St. Andrews, although it could not be more than a day or two.

34. Shaw, *Major Barbara*, 56.

35. Ibid., 57.

36. Wisenthal, "Marriage of Contraries," 196.

37. A. M. Gibbs, "Action and Meaning in *Major Barbara*," 158.

38. Matheson, "Lure of Power," 287.

39. Turco, *Shaw's Moral Vision*, 226.

40. Ishii, "Two Political Implications," 22. Even Shaw himself seems quite impressed with his character. In a letter to Louis Calvert, whom he was trying to persuade to take the part of Undershaft, Shaw says, "the part of the millionaire cannon founder is becoming more and more formidable. [. . .] Undershaft is diabolically subtle, gentle, self-possessed, powerful, stupendous [. . .] there are the makings of ten Hamlets and six Othellos in his mere leavings" (Herold, "Writing," 37, quoting E. J. West's 1958 book, *Shaw on Theatre*, 106–7).

41. Jordan, "Theme and Character," 473.

42. Turco, *Shaw's Moral Vision*, 206.

43. Matheson, "Lure of Power," 293.

44. Turco, *Shaw's Moral Vision*, 211.

45. Shaw, preface to *Major Barbara*, 118.

46. Wisenthal, "Marriage of Contraries," 200.

47. Crompton, *Shaw the Dramatist*, 116.

48. Wisenthal, "Marriage of Contraries," 198.

49. Shaw, preface to *Major Barbara*, 122.

50. Shaw, *Major Barbara*, 64.

51. Shaw, preface to *Major Barbara*, 122.

52. Shaw, *Man and Superman*, 391.

53. Ibid., 393.

54. Shaw, *Major Barbara*, 1.

55. Crompton, *Shaw the Dramatist*, 106.

56. Ibid., 107.

57. The fact is, education plays a rather substantial role in the play, but Shaw himself seems to have a rather ambivalent attitude toward learning—having on the one hand been deprived of an advanced formal education and, on the other, becoming one of the most well-read persons of his age by dint of his own efforts in the Reading Room of the British Museum. Formal education, he attacks; erudition he values. This ambivalence may be seen in his treatment of Cusins.

58. Shaw, *Major Barbara*, 50.

59. Ibid., 61.

60. Ibid., 8.

61. Ibid., 3.

62. Ibid.

63. Ibid.

64. Jordan, "Theme and Character," 475.

65. Diane Long Hoeveler, "Shaw's Vision of God in *Major Barbara*," 17.

66. Wisenthal, "Marriage of Contraries," 206.

67. Gibbs, "Action and Meaning," 162.

68. Matheson, "Lure of Power," 288.

69. Gibbs, "Action and Meaning," 164.

70. Jordan, "Theme and Character," 475.

71. Wisenthal, "Marriage of Contraries," 211.

72. Matheson, "Lure of Power," 290.

73. Jordan, "Theme and Character," 478.

74. Ibid., 477.

75. Gibbs, "Action and Meaning," 164.

76. Ishii, "Two Political Implications," 17–18.

77. Wisenthal, "Marriage of Contraries," 209.

78. Jordan, "Theme and Character," 480.

79. Shaw, *Major Barbara*, 63.

80. Ibid.

81. Crompton, *Shaw the Dramatist*, 122.

82. Shaw, *Major Barbara*, 69.

83. Ibid., 71.

Chapter 7. *Misalliance*: Gardens and Books as the Means to New Dramatic Forms

1. George Bernard Shaw, *Misalliance*, 3.

2. Jane Ann Crum, "Stanley Kauffmann on the Unknown Shaw: *You Never Can Tell, Misalliance, Androcles and the Lion, Too True to Be Good*," 36.

3. Ibid., 32.

4. Ibid. Kauffmann talks pointedly about one experience when he stage-managed *Misalliance* and saw about twenty-five performances of it over the course of some months. "And it was possible after all those rehearsals and performances to hear that the play is really built musically, that it exists in large phrases. One episode leads to another, like variations on themes. There are very few plays by Shaw in which his background of musical training and sensibility is more patent, operative, and beneficial" (ibid., 38).

5. Holroyd, *Bernard Shaw: The One-Volume Definitive Edition*, 241.

6. Ibid., 247.

7. Rodelle Weintraub, "Johnny's Dream," 174–75. Weintraub quotes from Walter Stewart and Lucy Freeman, *The Secret of Dreams* (New York: Macmillan, 1972), 152.

8. Crum, "Stanley Kauffmann," 42.

9. Weintraub, "Johnny's Dream," 179.

10. Shaw, *Misalliance*, 3.

11. Ibid.

12. Ibid.

13. Ibid.

14. Ibid.

15. Ibid.

16. Holroyd, *Bernard Shaw: The One-Volume Definitive Edition*, 247.

17. Crum, "Stanley Kauffmann," 37.

18. Shaw, *Misalliance*, 47.

19. Ibid., 55.

20. Ibid., 101.

21. Ibid., 47.

22. Ibid.

23. Ibid., 53.

24. Weintraub, "Johnny's Dream," 175.

25. Ibid.

26. Holroyd, *Bernard Shaw: The One-Volume Definitive Edition*, 248.

27. Ibid., 249.

28. Shaw, *Misalliance*, 34.

29. Ibid., 61.

30. Ibid., 100.

31. Ibid., 48.

32. Ibid., 49.

33. Ibid., 61.

34. Ibid., 62.

35. Ibid., 64.

36. Ibid.

37. Ibid., 76.

38. Ibid., 77.

39. Ibid.

40. Ibid., 94.

41. Ibid.

42. Ibid., 94–95.

43. Ibid., 95.

44. Ibid.

45. Ibid., 96.

46. Ibid., 54.

47. Ibid.

48. Ibid., 3.

49. Ibid., 12.

50. Ibid.

51. Ibid., 68–69.

52. Strong elements of postmodernism appear to be present in *Misalliance*. See Tony J. Stafford, "Postmodern Elements in Shaw's *Misalliance*."

53. Holroyd points out that Shaw himself informed the actor Louis Calvert that Tarleton is "a comic Undershaft" (*Bernard Shaw: The One-Volume Definitive Edition*, 245).

54. Shaw, *Misalliance*, 8.

55. Ibid., 31.

56. Weintraub says that the play "pokes rather gentle good-humored fun at the new mercantile class which in the nineteenth century had achieved great wealth and influence. [. . .] Tarleton's rapid rise from humble beginnings to the ownership of a luxurious country estate [. . .] reflects the success of those extraordinary nineteenth-century entrepreneurs" ("Johnny's Dream," 172).

57. Shaw, *Misalliance*, 25.

58. Ibid., 26.

59. Ibid., 25.

60. Ibid., 45.

61. Ibid., 28.

62. Ibid., 32.

63. Ibid., 28.

64. Ibid.

65. Crum, "Stanley Kauffmann," 37.

66. A. M. Gibbs, *Bernard Shaw: A Life*, 115.

67. Ibid., 116.

68. Ibid., 171–73.

69. Allan Chappelow, *Shaw, "The Chucker-Out": A Biographical Exposition and Critique*, 393.

70. Shaw, *Misalliance*, 22.

71. Shaw, *Collected Letters*, 2: 729.

72. Shaw, *Misalliance*, 123.

73. Ibid.

74. Ibid., 24.

75. Shaw, *Arms and the Man*, 21.

76. Shaw, *Misalliance*, 8–9.

77. Ibid., 67.

78. Ibid., 71.

79. Ibid., 90.

80. Ibid., 4.

81. Ibid., 28.

82. Ibid., 29.

83. Ibid., 30.

84. Ibid.

85. Ibid., 92–93.

86. Holroyd explains that *Misalliance* was written to be part of a repertory scheme to open in the West End of London, and the man behind this enterprise was the powerful Broadway impresario Charles Frohman, and it so happened that Frohman "worshipped mothers and children." Accordingly, Shaw had deliberately chosen the theme of parents and children because it was close to Frohman's heart" (*Bernard Shaw: The One-Volume Definitive Edition*, 243). Robert Everding, in "Bernard Shaw, Miss Alliance, and Miss Cotterill" (*English Language Notes* 25, no. 4 [June 1988]: 73–81) points out that in 1919 Shaw stated that "Tarleton is a serious parental study" (77; quoted from George Bernard Shaw, *Collected Letters*, vol. 3, *1911–1925*, 651), and that in this play "Shaw explored fully for the first time the parent-child relationship" (80) and that it would "provide material for subsequent plays and essays" (80).

87. Chappelow, *Shaw, "The Chucker-Out,"* 35.

88. Ibid.

89. Gibbs, *Shaw: A Life*, 221.

90. Shaw, *Mrs. Warren's Profession*, 174–75.

91. Ibid., 244.

92. Ibid., 280.

93. Ibid., 284.

94. Ibid.

95. Ibid., 286.

96. Shaw, *Misalliance*, 42.

97. Ibid., 44.

98. Ibid.

99. Ibid.

100. Ibid.

101. Ibid., 44.

102. Chappelow, *Shaw, "The Chucker-Out,"* 206.

103. Gibbs, *Shaw: A Life*, 378.

104. Ibid., 380.

105. Ibid., 378.

106. Chappelow, *Shaw, "The Chucker-Out,"* 210.

107. Shaw, *Misalliance*, 26. In 1890, long before he wrote *Misalliance*, Shaw gave an address to the Fabian Society, on December 19, titled "Socialism and Human Nature" in which he describes "our typical successful man" as "an odious person, vulgar, thick-skinned" but also "religious, charitable, patriotic, and full to the neck of ideals" (Chappelow, *Shaw, "The Chucker-Out,"* 234). He goes on to admit that if one conversed with "these blackguards," one might find them to be "potentially decent enough fellows," and then, as though anticipating his creation of Tarleton some twenty years later, "fellows, who had found that the line of least resistance had led them to unintended enormities, and whose attempt to disguise those enormities from themselves by the clumsy but well meant hypocrisies of idealism showed that they had plenty of good in them" (ibid., 234). It is an eerie foreshadowing of the maker of Tarleton's Underwear.

108. Shaw, *Misalliance*, 26.

109. Ibid.

110. Ibid.

111. Ibid., 28.

112. Ibid., 32.

113. Ibid., 54.

114. Ibid., 56.

115. Ibid., 57.

116. Ibid.

117. Ibid.

118. Ibid., 90–91.

Chapter 8. *Heartbreak House*: "A Long Garden Seat on the West"

1. George Bernard Shaw, *Heartbreak House*, in *Bernard Shaw's Plays*, 144. Future citations are from this edition.

2. Ibid., 135.

3. Ibid., 75.

4. A. M. Gibbs, "*Heartbreak House*: Chamber of Echoes," 115.

5. Stanley Weintraub, *Journey to Heartbreak: The Crucible Years of Bernard Shaw, 1914–1918*, 180.

6. Crompton, *Shaw the Dramatist*, 168.

7. Shaw, *Heartbreak House*, 75.

8. Ibid., 75–76.

9. Ibid., 93.

10. Ibid., 119.

11. Ibid., 128.

12. Ibid., 145.

13. Richard Hornby, "The Symbolic Action of *Heartbreak House*," 21. Hornby also points out that "this is an amazing passage for Shaw" and that "there is no attempt at prettiness, but instead a nice tension [is created] between the sublime and the colloquial" (21).

14. Shaw, *Heartbreak House*, 96.

15. Ibid. 98.

16. Ibid., 135.

17. Ibid.

18. Turco, *Shaw's Moral Vision*, 232.

19. Roger B. Wilkenfeld, "Perpetual Motion in *Heartbreak House*," 325.

20. Peters, "*Heartbreak House*: Shaw's Ship of Fools," 272.

21. Shaw, *Heartbreak House*, 83.

22. Ibid., 95.

23. Ibid., 108.

24. Ibid., 112.

25. Ibid., 134.

26. Turco, *Shaw's Moral Vision*, 236.

27. Ibid., 242.

28. Ibid., 81.

29. Ibid., 75.

30. In addition to all the recognized sources in the play, ranging in time from Homer to Chekhov, the present study has identified several other literary echoes in *Heartbreak House*, which no one seems to have noticed, such as Walt Whitman in Ellie's "O Captain, my captain" (Shaw, *Heartbreak House*, 145), *Midsummer Night's Dream* in "with their eyes in a fine frenzy rolling" (84), *Othello* in "is there no thunder in heaven," and others. Also, no one seems to have connected Marcus Darnley's wearing an Arab costume with Othello, whose identity he assumes as a romantic adventurer. Ironically, it is Hesione who insists on Hector's wearing the Arab costume, even though she has rejected Othello as a fraud. One wonders if this may say something about her unconscious attitude toward her husband.

31. In a similar vein, Turco declares that the "entire play is a portrayal of the artistic imagination" (*Shaw's Moral Vision*, 242).

32. Shaw, *Heartbreak House*, 104.

33. Ibid., 126.

34. Ibid., 136.

35. Ibid., 113.

36. Ibid.

37. Ibid.

38. Ibid.
39. Ibid., 114.
40. Ibid.
41. Crompton, *Shaw the Dramatist*, 160.
42. Hornby, "Symbolic Action," 17.
43. Crompton, *Shaw the Dramatist*, 161.
44. Shaw, *Heartbreak House*, 132.
45. Ibid., 134.
46. Ibid.
47. Ibid., 115.
48. Ibid.
49. Ibid.
50. Ibid.
51. Ibid.
52. Ibid.
53. Ibid., 124.
54. Ibid., 141.
55. Ibid., 126.
56. Ibid.
57. Ibid.
58. Ibid.
59. Crompton, *Shaw the Dramatist*, 164.
60. Shaw, *Heartbreak House*, 107.
61. Ibid., 110.
62. Ibid., 116.
63. Ibid.
64. Ibid.
65. Ibid., 117.
66. Ibid.
67. Ibid., 96.
68. Ibid., 98.
69. Peters, *"Heartbreak House,"* 279.
70. Daniel Leary, *"Heartbreak House: A Dramatic Epic,"* 12.
71. Shaw, *Heartbreak House*, 135.
72. Ibid.
73. Ibid.
74. Ibid.
75. Peters, *"Heartbreak House,"* 280.
76. Fred E. Stockholder, "A Schopenhauerian Reading of Heartbreak House," 38.
77. Crompton, *Shaw the Dramatist*, 165.
78. Peters, *"Heartbreak House,"* 280.
79. Wilkenfeld, "Perpetual Motion," 333.
80. Hornby, "Symbolic Action," 10.
81. Shaw, *Heartbreak House*, 135.

82. Ibid., 136.
83. Ibid., 142.
84. Ibid., 137.
85. Ibid., 140.
86. Ibid., 139.
87. Ibid., 140.
88. Ibid., 135.
89. Ibid., 147.
90. Ibid., 148.

Chapter 9. *Back to Methuselah*: The Original Garden and a Library Too

1. Maurice Valency, *The Cart and the Trumpet*, 349.
2. Ibid.
3. Julie Sparks, "Playwrights' Progress: The Evolution of the Play Cycle, from Shaw's 'Pentateuch' to *Angels in America*," 179.
4. Margery M. Morgan, *The Shavian Playground: An Exploration of the Art of George Bernard Shaw*, 221.
5. Ibid., 238.
6. Crompton, *Shaw the Dramatist*, 192.
7. Valency, *Cart*, 366.
8. Ibid., 354.
9. James Agate, *Sunday Times*, February 24, 1924, 4, reprinted in T. F. Evans, ed., *Shaw: The Critical Heritage*, 272.
10. Morgan, *Shavian Playground*, 238.
11. Desmond MacCarthy, *New Statesman*, July 9, 1921, 17: 384, in Evans, *Critical Heritage*, 265.
12. Sparks, "Playwrights' Progress," 179.
13. Ibid., 180.
14. Ibid.
15. J. C. Squire, *Observer*, June 26, 1921, 6786, 4, in Evans, *Critical Heritage*, 262.
16. Ibid.
17. Valency, *Cart*, 350.
18. Ibid.
19. Ibid.
20. Ibid.
21. Ibid., 351.
22. Ibid., 350.
23. Ibid., 356.
24. Squire, in Evans, *Critical Heritage*, 264.
25. Crompton, *Shaw the Dramatist*, 169.
26. Ibid.
27. George Bernard Shaw, *Back to Methuselah: A Metabiological Pentateuch*, 1.
28. Ibid.
29. Ibid., 5.

30. Ibid.

31. Ibid., 20.

32. Ibid., 1.

33. Ibid., 21.

34. Ibid., 22.

35. Ibid.

36. Ibid., 29.

37. Ibid., 38.

38. Ibid., 9.

39. Christopher L.C.E. Witcombe, "Eve and Lilith," 3.

40. Ibid., 4.

41. Ibid.

42. Ibid., 5.

43. Ibid.

44. "Dante Gabriel Rossetti's Poem 'Lilith,' Later Published as 'Body's Beauty' (1968)."

45. Robert Browning, "Adam, Lilith, and Eve."

46. Shaw, *Candida*, 157.

47. Since Shaw creates so many strong women in his plays, many of whom seem to partake of various superman traits, and since Shaw himself seems to possess certain superman qualities himself, one wonders if Shaw might not be disguising himself in some of his female characters. It is an interesting theory for another research project.

48. Shaw, *Back to Methuselah*, 24.

49. Ibid., 25.

50. Ibid., 26.

51. Ibid.

52. Ibid., 27.

53. Ibid., 41.

54. Ibid.

55. Ibid.

56. Ibid., 44–45.

57. Ibid., 49.

58. Ibid., 55. This passage not only echoes the famous conclusion in *Candide* ("il faut cultiver notre jardin"), but also foreshadows the discussion of Voltaire by Pygmalion in the fifth part, *As Far as Thought Can Reach*.

59. Ibid., 70.

60. Ibid., 84.

61. Ibid., 85.

62. Ibid.

63. Ibid., 88.

64. Ibid., 87.

65. Ibid., 222.

66. Ibid., 225.

67. Ibid., 228.

68. Ibid., 230.

69. Ibid., 298.

70. Ibid., 297.

71. Rhodes, *Birmingham Post,* October 13, 1923, 20388, 10, reprinted in Evans, *Critical Heritage,* 270.

72. Squire, in Evans, *Critical Heritage,* 263.

73. Shaw, *Back to Methuselah,* 298.

74. Ibid., 299.

75. Ibid., 300.

76. Ibid.

77. Ibid.

78. Shaw, *Man and Superman,* 310.

BIBLIOGRAPHY

Adams, Elsie. "Bernard Shaw's Pre-Raphaelite Drama." *PMLA: Publications of the Modern Language Association of America* 81, no 5 (October 1966): 428–38.

Adler, Jacob H. "Ibsen, Shaw, and *Candida*." *Journal of English and Germanic Philology* 59 (1960): 50–58.

Bentley, Eric. *Bernard Shaw.* New York: Applause Theatre and Cinema Books, 2002.

Bergman, Herbert. "The Comedy in *Candida*." *Shavian: The Journal of Bernard Shaw* 4 (1972): 161–69.

Berst, Charles. "The Craft of *Candida*." *College Literature* 1 (1974): 157–73.

———. "Romance and Reality in *Arms and the Man*." *Modern Language Quarterly* 27 (1966): 197–211.

Bloy, Marjorie. "John Bright (1811–1889)." *A Web of English History.* http://www.historyhome.co.uk/people/bright.htm. Accessed 11 January 2013.

———. "Richard Cobden (1804–1865)." *A Web of English History.* http://www.historyhome.co.uk/people/cobden.htm. Accessed 11 January 2013.

Browning, Robert. "Adam, Lilith, and Eve." In *The Works of Robert Browning,* ed. F. G. Kenyon, 10: 25. New York: AMS Press, 1966.

Carpenter, Charles. *Bernard Shaw and the Art of Destroying Ideals: The Early Plays.* Milwaukee: University of Wisconsin Press, 1969.

Chappelow, Allan. *Shaw, "The Chucker-Out": A Biographical Exposition and Critique.* New York: AMS Press, 1971.

Churchill, Caryl. *Serious Money.* In *Plays 2: Softcops; Top Girls; Fen; Serious Money,* 196–309. London: Methuen Drama, 1996.

Conolly, Leonard. "Who Was Phillipa Summers? Reflections on Vivie Warren's Cambridge." *SHAW: The Annual of Bernard Shaw Studies* 25 (2005): 89–95.

Crompton, Louis. Introduction to *Arms and the Man.* By George Bernard Shaw. Indianapolis: Bobbs-Merrill, 1969.

———. *Shaw the Dramatist.* Lincoln: University of Nebraska Press, 1969.

Crum, Jane Ann. "Stanley Kauffmann on the Unknown Shaw: *You Never Can*

Tell, Misalliance, Androcles and the Lion, Too True to Be Good." *SHAW: The Annual of Bernard Shaw Studies* 7 (1987): 31–44.

"Dante Gabriel Rossetti's Poem 'Lilith,' Later Published as 'Body's Beauty' (1968)" *Feminism and Women's Studies.* http://feminism.eserver.org/theory/papers/lilith/bodybeau.html. Accessed 25 March 2013.

Deltcheva, Roumiana. "East Central Europe as a Politically Correct Scapegoat: The Case of Bulgaria." *CLCWeb: Comparative Literature and Culture* 1, no. 2 (June 1999). http://docs.lib.purdue.edu/clcweb/vol1/iss2/4. Accessed 15 June 2009.

Dicey, Edward. *The Peasant State: An Account of Bulgaria in 1894.* London: John Murray, 1894.

Doan, William J. "*Candida:* The Eye on Duty." *SHAW: The Annual of Bernard Shaw Studies* 22 (2002): 131–47.

Dukore, Bernard. "The Ablest Man in Bulgaria." *SHAW: The Annual of Bernard Shaw Studies* 22 (2002): 67–82.

———. "*Widowers' Houses:* A Question of Genre." *Modern Drama* 17 (1974): 27–32.

Emmett, V. J. "Roebuck Ramsden's Study: Shaw as Philosophical Conservative." *Journal of Irish Literature* 11, no. 3 (1982): 103–8.

Evans, T. F., ed. *Shaw: The Critical Heritage.* London: Routledge and Kegan Paul, 1976.

Everding, Robert. "Bernard Shaw, Miss Alliance, and Miss Cotterill." *English Language Notes* 25, no. 4 (June 1988): 73–81.

Frye, Northrop. *Words with Power: Being a Second Study of "The Bible and Literature."* San Diego: Harcourt Brace Jovanovich, Publishers, 1990.

Ganz, Arthur. *George Bernard Shaw.* New York: Grove Press, 1983.

"George Eliot: Biography: From Mary Anne Evans to George Eliot." University of Virginia Library Digital Curation Services Etext Projects. http://web.archive.org/web/20070105175343/http://etext.lib.virginia.edu/collections/projects/eliot/middlemarch/bio.html. Accessed 25 March 2013.

Gibbs, A. M. "Action and Meaning in *Major Barbara.*" In *The Art and Mind of Shaw: Essays in Criticism,* 153–67. New York: St. Martin's Press, 1983.

———. *Bernard Shaw: A Life.* Gainesville: University Press of Florida, 2005.

———. "*Heartbreak House:* Chamber of Echoes." *SHAW: The Annual of Bernard Shaw Studies* 13 (1993): 113–32.

"Herbert Spencer." *The Internet Encyclopedia of Philosophy.* http://www.iep.utm.edu/s/spencer/. Accessed 23 February 2013.

Herold, Larry. "Writing Was Only Step One: Bernard Shaw's Immersion in the Premiere of *Major Barbara.*" *Independent Shavian* 42, nos. 1–2 (2004): 35–43.

Higgs, Calvin T., Jr. "Shaw's Use of Vergil's *Aeneid* in *Arms and the Man.*" *Shaw Review* 19 (1976): 2–16.

"Hippolyte Delaroche." *Catholic Encyclopedia.* http://www.newadvent.org/cathen/04691a.htm. Accessed 11 January 2013.

Hoeveler, Diane Long. "Shaw's Vision of God in *Major Barbara*." *Independent Shavian* 17 (1979): 16–18.

Holroyd, Michael. *Bernard Shaw*. Vol. 2, *1898–1918: The Pursuit of Power*. New York: Random House, 1989.

———. *Bernard Shaw: The One-Volume Definitive Edition*. New York: Random House, 1997.

Hornby, Richard. "The Symbolic Action of *Heartbreak House*." *Drama Survey* 7 (1968–1969): 5–24.

Ishii, Michiyo. "Two Political Implications of Shaw's *Major Barbara*." *Studies in English Literature* (1987): 21–32.

"Jesse Ramsden." *History*. http://chem.ch.huji.ac.il/-eugeniik/history/ramsden.htm. Accessed 8 October 2004.

"John Roebuck." *Spartacus Educational*. http://www.spartacus.schoolnet.co.uk/PRroebuck.htm. Accessed 11 January 2013.

Jordan, Robert J. "Theme and Character in *Major Barbara*." *Texas Studies in Literature and Language* 12 (1970): 471–80.

King, Walter N. "The Rhetoric of *Candida*." *Modern Drama* 2 (1959): 71–83.

Laurence, Dan H. "Victorians Unveiled: Some Thoughts on *Mrs. Warren's Profession*." *SHAW: The Annual of Bernard Shaw Studies* 24 (2004): 38–45.

Lazenby, Walter. "Love and 'Vitality' in *Candida*." *Modern Drama* 20 (1977): 1–19.

Leary, Daniel. "*Heartbreak House*: A Dramatic Epic." *Independent Shavian* 37, nos. 1–2 (1999): 3–13.

Lucas, John. "Dickens and Shaw: Women and Marriage in *David Copperfield* and *Candida*." *Shaw Review* 22 (1979): 13–22.

MacCarthy, Fiona. "England's Michelangelo." *Guardian,* 6 August 2004. http://www.guardian.co.uk/artanddesign/2004/aug/07/art.art. Accessed 25 March 2013.

Marker, Frederick J. "Shaw's Early Play." In *The Cambridge Companion to George Bernard Shaw,* ed. Christopher Innes, 103–23. Cambridge: Cambridge University Press, 1998.

Marx, Leo. *The Machine in the Garden: Technology and the Pastoral Ideal in America*. London: Oxford University Press, 1964.

Matheson, T. J. "The Lure of Power and the Triumph of Capital: An Ironic Reading of *Major Barbara*." *English Studies in Canada* 12, no. 3 (1986): 285–300.

McDowell, Frederick P. W. "*Widowers' Houses*: A Play for the 1890s and the 1990s." *SHAW: The Annual of Bernard Shaw Studies* 14 (1994): 231–40.

Morgan, Margery M. *The Shavian Playground: An Exploration of the Art of George Bernard Shaw*. London: Methuen, 1972.

Morrison, Kristin. "Horrible Flesh and Blood." *Theatre Notebook: A Journal of the History and Technique of the British Theatre* 35 (1981): 7–9.

Mudford, Peter. "*Mrs. Warren's Profession*." *The Shavian: The Journal of the Shaw Society* 6, no. 5 (1978): 4–10.

Nelson, Raymond S. "Shaw's *Widowers' Houses*," *Research Studies* 37 (1969): 27–37.

Nethercot, Arthur H. "The Truth about *Candida*." *PMLA: Publication of the Modern Language Association* 64, no. 4 (September 1949): 639–47.

Ortega y Gasset, José. *The Revolt of the Masses*. Authorized translation from the Spanish. New York: Norton, 1932.

Pagliaro, Harold. "Truncated Love in *Candida* and *Heartbreak House*." *SHAW: The Annual of Bernard Shaw Studies* 24 (2004): 204–14.

Perrine, Laurence. "Shaw's *Arms and the Man*." *Explicator* 15 (1957): item 56.

Peters, Sally. "*Heartbreak House*: Shaw's Ship of Fools." *Modern Drama* 21 (1978): 267–86.

———. *See also* Vogt, Sally Peters.

Pichanick, Valerie Kossew. *Harriet Martineau: The Woman and Her Work, 1802–76*. Ann Arbor: University of Michigan Press, 1980.

Sauer, David K. "'Only a Woman' in *Arms and the Man*." *Shaw: Annual of Bernard Shaw Studies* 15 (1995): 151–66.

Schechner, Richard. *Performance Studies: An Introduction*. London: Routledge, 2003.

Shaw, George Bernard. *Arms and the Man*. Ed. Louis Crompton. Indianapolis: Bobbs-Merrill, 1969.

———. *Back to Methuselah: A Metabiological Pentateuch*. New York: Brentano's, 1922.

———. *Bernard Shaw's Plays: Major Barbara; Heartbreak House; Saint Joan; Too True to Be Good*. Ed. Warren S. Smith. New York: W. W. Norton, 1970.

———. *Collected Letters*. Vol. 2, *1898–1910*. Ed. Dan H. Laurence. New York: Dodd, Mead, 1972.

———. *Collected Letters*. Vol. 3, *1911–1925*. Ed. Dan H. Laurence. New York: Viking, 1985.

———. *Misalliance*. New York: Brentano's, 1917.

———. *Mrs. Warren's Profession*. In *Plays Unpleasant: Widowers' Houses; The Philanderer; Mrs Warren's Profession*. Harmondsworth: Penguin Books, 1946.

———. *Plays Pleasant: Arms and the Man; Candida; The Man of Destiny; You Never Can Tell*. Ed. Dan H. Laurence. London: Penguin Books, 1957.

———. *Plays Unpleasant: Widowers' Houses; The Philanderer; Mrs Warren's Profession*. Ed. Dan H. Laurence. New York: Penguin Books, 1981.

———. Preface to *Major Barbara*. In *The Complete Prefaces of Bernard Shaw*, 115–37. London: Paul Hamlyn, 1965.

———. *Shaw on Theatre*. Ed. E. J. West. New York: Hill and Wang, 1958.

———. *The Theatre of Bernard Shaw*. Ed. Alan S. Downer. Vol. 1. New York: Dodd, Mead, 1969.

Sparks, Julie. "Playwrights' Progress: The Evolution of the Play Cycle, from Shaw's

'Pentateuch' to *Angels in America.*" *SHAW: The Annual of Bernard Shaw Studies* 25 (2005): 179–200.

Stafford, Tony J. "*Mrs Warren's Profession:* In the Garden of Respectability." *SHAW: The Annual of Bernard Shaw Studies* 2 (1982): 3–11.

———. "Postmodern Elements in Shaw's *Misalliance.*" *SHAW: The Annual of Bernard Shaw Studies* 29 (2009): 176–88.

"Stewart Headlam." *Spartacus Educational.* http://www.spartacus.schoolnet. co.uk/REheadlam.htm. Accessed 11 January 2013.

Stockholder, Fred E. "A Schopenhauerian Reading of *Heartbreak House.*" *Shaw Review* 19 (1976): 22–43.

"Thomas Henry Huxley (1825–1895)." *BBC History: Historic Figures.* http://bbc. co.uk/history/historic_figures/huxley_thomas_henry.shtml. Accessed 11 January 2013.

Turco, Alfred, Jr. *Shaw's Moral Vision: The Self and Salvation.* Ithaca: Cornell University Press, 1976.

Valency, Maurice. *The Cart and the Trumpet: The Plays of George Bernard Shaw.* New York: Oxford University Press, 1971.

Vogeler, Martha. "*Widowers' Houses* and the London County Council." *Independent Shavian* 24 (1986): 3–11.

Vogt, Sally Peters. "Ann and Superman: Type and Archetype." In *George Bernard Shaw's Man and Superman,* ed. Harold Bloom, 105–23. New York: Chelsea House Publishers, 1987.

———. *See also* Peters, Sally.

Wasserman, Marie Parker. "Vivie Warren: A Psychological Study." In *Fabian Feminist: Bernard Shaw and Women,* ed. Rodelle Weintraub, 168–73. University Park: Pennsylvania State University Press, 1977.

Weintraub, Rodelle. "Johnny's Dream in *Misalliance.*" *SHAW: The Annual of Bernard Shaw Studies* 7 (1987): 171–86.

Weintraub, Stanley. *Journey to Heartbreak: The Crucible Years of Bernard Shaw, 1914–1918.* New York: Weybright and Talley, 1971.

Weiss, Samuel A. "Shaw, *Arms and the Man,* and the Bulgarians." *SHAW: The Annual of Bernard Shaw Studies* 10 (1990): 27–44.

White, Patrick. "*Candida:* Bernard Shaw's Chaucerian Drama." *SHAW: The Annual of Bernard Shaw Studies* 12 (1992): 213–28.

Wilkenfeld, Roger B. "Perpetual Motion in *Heartbreak House.*" *Texas Studies in Literature and Language: A Journal of the Humanities* 13 (1971): 321–35.

Williams, Raymond. *Drama in Performance.* New York: Basic Books, 1968.

Winsten, Stephen. *Jesting Apostle: The Life of Bernard Shaw* London: Dutton, 1956.

Wisenthal, J. L. "The Cosmology of *Man and Superman.*" *Modern Drama* 14 (1971): 298–306.

———. "The Marriage of Contraries: *Major Barbara.*" In *Modern Critical Views:*

George Bernard Shaw, ed. Harold Bloom, 189–213. New York: Chelsea House Publishers, 1987.

Witcombe, Christopher L.C.E. "Eve and Lilith." *Eve and the Identity of Women.* http://witcombe.sbc.edu/eve-women/7evelilith.html. Accessed 11 January 2013.

Woodfield, James. "Shaw's *Candida:* A Comedy." *English Studies in Canada* 16, no. 4 (1990): 445–62.

———. "Shaw's *Widowers' Houses:* Comedy for Socialism's Sake." *SHAW: The Annual of Bernard Shaw Studies* 11 (1991): 47–64.

INDEX

Industrial revolution, 64–65

In the Beginning (Shaw), 115–16, 120; thistle motif of, 121. See also *Back to Methuselah*

Ishii, Michiyo, 80, 84

Jacob's ladder, 69, 144n83

Jordan, Robert, 74, 84

Jung, Carl, 56, 129; archetypes of, 72

Kauffmann, Stanley, 87–88, 89, 95, 101, 148n4

King, Walter, 44, 45

Kirshenblatt-Gimblett, Barbara, 7

Langner, Lawrence, 111

Laurence, Dan, 23, 24

Laurentian Library, 6

Lazenby, Walter, 45

Lewes, George Henry, 58

Libraries: in British society, 6; elements comprising, 4; as extensions of self, 56; importance for Shaw, 3; personal, 6; semiotics of, 5–6; symbolism of, 5; in Western culture, 5–6, 20

Libraries, Shaw's, xi–xii; appearances in, 82; of *Arms and the Man*, 2, 4, 34–35, 43, 129, 137nn38,44, 138n80, 141n5; of *Back to Methuselah*, 113, 119; of *Candida*, 2, 44, 49–51, 52, 54, 129, 130, 140n49; corruption in, 76; definition of, 76–77; frequency of appearances of, 2; of *Gospel of the Brothers Barnabas*, 3, 119; of *Heartbreak House*, 4; of *Major Barbara*, 2, 76, 82, 85–86, 129, 130; in *Man and Superman*, 2, 4, 55–56, 59, 61, 68, 73; as metaphors, 128; in *Misalliance*, 93; and mocking of idealism, 2; role in character development of, 22; romanticized, 38; social symbolism of, 6; as symbolization of hypocrisy, 10, 19, 20, 22, 126; in *Widowers' Houses*, 2, 9, 19–21, 39, 125–26

Life Force, 2, 111; in *Back to Methuselah*, 113; in *Candida*, 118; garden setting of, 70, 71, 72; in *Major Barbara*, 80; in *Man and Superman*, 59, 61, 67, 70, 73, 118, 127; in

Misalliance, 91, 99, 100; women's, 118, 123, 128

Lilith: in *As Far as Thought Can Reach*, 122; in *Back to Methuselah*, 111, 114, 116–18; and Eve, 117, 118–19; myth of, 116–17; sexual power of, 122

London: East End, 47–48, 49, 50; parks of, 3–4, 47–48; Polytechnic Institute, 63; Tower Hamlets borough, 48, 50, 51; Victoria Park, 47–48, 50, 54, 130

Lucas, John, 45

MacCarthy, Desmond, 112

Machines: in American literature, 65; in *Man and Superman*, 62–67, 69–70; in Western culture, 65

Major Barbara (Shaw): appearances in, 83; book motif of, 83, 85; capitalism in, 2; critical opinion on, 74–75, 80, 83–84, 146n31; education in, 82–83, 147n57; gardens in, 76, 77–79; hypocrisy in, 83, 85, 86; irony in, 78, 79; library of, 2, 76, 82, 85–86, 129, 130; Life Force in, 80; money in, 75, 84, 85; poverty in, 75, 76, 77–78, 80–81, 84, 86; preface to, 74–75, 80, 81; stage directions of, 79; technology in, 143n44; themes of, 74; weather in, 77–78, 79; Will in, 81

Man and Superman (Shaw): Adam and Eve motif of, 69, 72–73; Alhambra in, 68, 144n74; book motif of, 61, 68; "Don Juan in Hell" scene, 81, 144n82; Edenic tree of, 62; gardens of, 61, 62–73, 144nn70,74; library of, 2, 4, 55–56, 59, 61, 68, 73, 141n5; Life Force in, 59, 61, 67, 70, 73, 118, 127; machines in, 62–67, 69–70; motor trip motif, 66; New Man in, 62–67; New Woman in, 63; performance values of, 127; progressivism in, 55–56, 57, 60; social status in, 70–71; spatial freedom in, 143n70; speed in, 65–66; stage descriptions of, 55, 60, 62, 68; technology in, 143n44

Marker, Frederick J., 10

Martineau, Harriet, 57

TONY JASON STAFFORD is professor of English at the University of Texas at El Paso, where he was recognized for fifty years of teaching. He has published articles in *Shaw: The Annual of Bernard Shaw Studies, Modern Drama, The Upstart Crow,* and other journals in dramatic literature studies.

*   *   *

The University Press of Florida is the scholarly publishing agency for the State University System of Florida, comprising Florida A&M University, Florida Atlantic University, Florida Gulf Coast University, Florida International University, Florida State University, New College of Florida, University of Central Florida, University of Florida, University of North Florida, University of South Florida, and University of West Florida.